LIGETI IN CONVERSATION

György Ligeti
(Photo: Peter Andersen)

GYÖRGY LIGETI
IN CONVERSATION

with
Péter Várnai
Josef Häusler
Claude Samuel
and himself

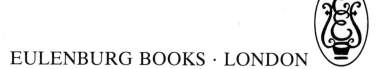

EULENBURG BOOKS · LONDON

This book first published 1983 by
Ernst Eulenburg Ltd
48 Great Marlborough Street, London W1V 2BN

Interviews originally published separately in:
1. Péter Várnai: *Beszélgetések Ligeti Györggyel*
   Zenemükiadó Vállalat, Budapest
   © 1979 Péter Várnai
2. O. Nordwall: *György Ligeti: eine Monographie*
   'Zwei Interviews mit György Ligeti' (Josef Häusler)
   © 1971 B. Schott's Söhne, Mainz
3. *Le Grand Macabre*
   'Entretien avec György Ligeti' (Claude Samuel)
   © 1981 Hubschmid & Bouret, Éditeurs, Paris
4. *Melos*, Dezember 1971
   'Fragen und Antworten von mir selbst'
   © 1971 B. Schott's Söhne, Mainz

English translations © 1983 Ernst Eulenburg Ltd, London

ISBN 0 903873 68 0

Phototypeset by Tradespools Ltd, Frome, Somerset
Printed by Page Bros (Norwich) Ltd, Norwich, England

CONTENTS

INTRODUCTION

György Ligeti was born on 28 May 1923 in the little Transylvanian town of Dicsöszentmárton, which is today known as Tîrnăveni in Romania. He went to secondary school in Klausenburg (Cluj), taking his final examination there in 1941. He remained for a further two years in Klausenburg, studying composition at the Conservatory under Ferenc Farkas, one of the most respected Hungarian composers at that time. Ligeti composed his first work at the age of fourteen, and between 1938 and 1943 in Klausenburg he wrote pieces for piano and other instruments, a string quartet, songs for voice and piano, unaccompanied choral works and an unfinished symphony. The first thing to be published was the song *Kineret* for mezzosoprano and piano, which appeared in Budapest in 1941.

As well as studying with Farkas in Klausenburg, Ligeti also took private lessons in 1942 and 1943 with the composer and pianist Pál Kadosa in Budapest; from 1945 until 1949 he studied at the Budapest Academy of Music under Sándor Veress, Pál Járdányi and Ferenc Farkas. After this he went on an extended tour of Romania, during which he noted down some hundreds of Transylvanian/Hungarian folk-songs. He was lecturer in harmony, counterpoint and musical analysis at the Budapest Academy of Music from 1950 to 1956. Two educational works on classical harmony, still used in Hungary today, are the products of this period.

Ligeti's creativity developed considerably during his time in Budapest, his chief inspirations being, as he himself admits, Bartók and Stravinsky. These two impelled him in varying directions, with the result that he produced, among many other things, two cantatas, numerous unaccompanied choral works, songs and piano pieces, a large number of settings of Hungarian and Romanian folk-songs and several orchestral works: among the latter *Víziók* in 1956, which was the first version of the first movement of *Apparitions*, completed two years later in the West. Ligeti considered only a few of his compositions up to 1956

7

worthy of publication. These included *Six Bagatelles* for wind quintet (1953), two unaccompanied choral pieces, *Night* and *Morning* (1955), and above all the String Quartet No.1, *Métamorphoses nocturnes* (1953–54).

When, after the Hungarian uprising of 1956, Ligeti came to the West and became acquainted with the latest trends in Western music, his composition took the definitive turn towards what we now know as 'typical Ligeti'. At first he was involved in 1957/58 with the work of the West German Studio for electronic music in Cologne, which resulted in his electronic works, *Glissandi* and *Artikulation*.

In the subsequent ten years (1959–69), Ligeti lived primarily in Vienna (he became an Austrian National in 1967). From 1959, he taught at the international holiday courses in Darmstadt, was visiting professor at the Academy of Music in Stockholm and directed courses in composition in Madrid, Bilthoven, at the Folkwang school in Essen and at Jyväskylä in Finland. The première of his first orchestral work completed in the West, *Apparitions* (1958–59), caused a sensation when given at the 1960 International Society for Contemporary Music Festival by Ernest Bour and the North German Radio Symphony Orchestra, and brought international recognition to the composer. Listeners were fascinated above all by its bold and original new sound world, which had nothing in common with the serialism prevalent at that time. *Apparitions* was the first of a long series of unusual compositions, each of them containing its own musical organism, preserving a relentless continuity of new musical ideas. Judged merely by the number of works produced, Ligeti's output is not exceptional; yet the spiritual and musical perception and concentration in each of his compositions reveal that even 'minor' pieces are the result of years of work. There is no such thing with him as casual composition.

His next work for large orchestra, *Atmosphères* (1961), had the same triumphal success as *Apparitions* at its first performance by Hans Rosbaud and the South West German Radio Orchestra at the Donaueschingen Music Festival of 1961: the audience demanded an encore of the whole piece. Ligeti's years in Vienna also produced *Volumina* for organ, *Aventures* and *Nouvelles Aventures* arranged for the stage (1962–65), the unaccompanied choral work *Lux aeterna*, the Cello Concerto, which had its première in Berlin with Siegfried Palm (1966) and – perhaps the climax of his creativity during these years – the Requiem for soprano and mezzosoprano, two mixed choirs and orchestra (1963–65), first heard in Stockholm in 1965 conducted by Michael Gielen.

Of his next piece, *Lontano* (far away, distant), Ligeti writes that it consists of 'simultaneous processes ... which ... superimpose themselves on one another and produce an imaginary perspective through all sorts of refraction and reflection. It reveals itself gradually to the listener, as though he were going into a dark room from bright sunlight and little by little becoming aware of the colours and contours.' The two following years produced *Ramifications* for string orchestra or twelve solo strings, commissioned for the Koussevitzky Music Foundation (1968–69): its title refers to the polyphonic technique of the part-writing which 'moves in different directions within a skein of tangled single parts'. [Ligeti] There were also *Ten Pieces* for wind quintet (1968), *Two Etudes* for organ (*Harmonies* 1967, and *Coulée* 1969); *Continuum* for harpsichord and one of his outstanding works, the five-movement String Quartet No.2 (1968) which was first performed by the Lasalle Quartet in Baden-Baden in December 1969.

From 1969 to 1973, Ligeti lived for the most part in Berlin, primarily as fellow of the German Academic Exchange Organization. In 1972 he was Composer in Residence at Stanford University in California. The main works from this period are the Chamber Concerto for thirteen instrumentalists (1969–70), *Melodien* for orchestra (1971), the Double Concerto for flute, oboe and orchestra (1972) and *Clocks and Clouds* for twelve-part female chorus and orchestra (1972–73), inspired by an article by Sir Karl Popper, 'Of Clouds and Clocks', and during which 'the musical happening consists mainly of processes in which clocks are dissolved into clouds, and clouds condense and materialize into clocks'.

In 1973 Ligeti accepted a professorship in composition at the Hamburg Academy of Music and has lived subsequently in Hamburg and Vienna. Between 1973 and 1974 he composed *San Francisco Polyphony* for orchestra, which is, as it were, a terminus of the stylistic line of the Wind Quintet pieces and *Melodien* in which the 'new' polyphony towards which the composer was striving from the middle of the '60s arrives at its consummate form. In 1973 Ligeti directed a course in composition at the Berkshire Music Center in Tanglewood (USA), and in 1974 at the Accademia Chigiana in Siena. In 1976 Leslie Megahey made a fifty-minute television documentary about Ligeti for the BBC.

Ligeti wrote the three pieces for two pianos, *Monument, Selbstportrait, Bewegung* also in 1976: they were performed for the first time by Alfons and Aloys Kontarsky in Cologne in May that year. 'The pieces were conceived totally from the premiss that two pianists will be performing: on the one hand, two similar instruments with the same tone-colour blend into one indissoluble sonorous unity; on the other, the fact that two independent performers are interpreting the music makes possible the intricate polyrhythm and metric shiftings.'

Ligeti devoted the years 1974–77 to writing his first full-length opera, *Le Grand Macabre*, which had its première on 12 April 1978 at the Royal Opera House in Stockholm. The performance was conducted by Elgar Howarth, produced by Michael Meschke and the décor and costumes were designed by Aliute Meczies. The first performance in Germany took place on 15 October 1978 at the Hamburg State Opera House, once more under the musical direction of Elgar Howarth. In May 1979 it had premières in Saarbrücken and Bologna, in February 1980 in Nuremberg, in March 1981 at the Opéra in Paris and in December 1982 at the English National Opera in London. And in the year of its first performance there appeared too 'Scenes and Interludes from *Le Grand Macabre*' for four singers, mixed choir ad lib and orchestra.

After two pieces for harpsichord, *Hungarian Rock* for Elisabeth Chojnacka and *Passacaglia ungherese* for Eva Nordwall, his next major work was the Trio for violin, horn and piano (1982), first played in August 1982 at the Bergedorf Castle concerts by Saschko Gawriloff (violin), Hermann Baumann (horn) and Eckart Besch (piano). Ligeti wrote the work in homage to Johannes Brahms, 'whose Horn Trio remains unequalled of its kind in the musical heavens. Nevertheless, there are neither quotations, nor direct influences of the music of Brahms: my trio is – in construction and expression – music for our time.' In 1982 Ligeti also composed *Drei Phantasien* for sixteen-part unaccompanied choir on poems by Friedrich Hölderlin, with a first performance planned for 26 September 1983 by the Stockholm Radio Choir under Eric Ericson. In 1983 he composed *Magyar Etüdök* (Hungarian Studies) for unaccompanied choir on poems of Sándor Weöres. At the time of writing (1983) Ligeti is working on a Piano Concerto, dedicated to Mario di Bonaventura.

Ever since taking up his first position at the Budapest Academy of Music, Ligeti has always been much sought after as a teacher: he has directed courses in composition, has been visiting professor at universities and academies. He is always willing to share his knowledge and his experience with young composers. He is deeply respected by his pupils, even though he demands exacting standards of application and self-criticism. Many writings about music have resulted from his passion for teaching and his concern to clarify complex musical questions, including those relevant to his own works: among these writings are those based on his extensive research into the work of Anton von Webern and Pierre Boulez and – invaluable for the appreciation of his own music – analyses and descriptions of his methods of work for almost all his compositions.

György Ligeti has been awarded many prizes and laurels, among them the membership of the German order 'Pour le mérite' in 1975. There have also been more and more concerts and festivals devoted to his works, such as the three concerts comprising a 'Journée Ligeti' at the Semaines Musicales in Paris in 1969, a 'Ligeti Festival' at Stanford, California in 1972, Ligeti concerts in Vienna and Stockholm in 1973, Ligeti evenings in London (Bach Festival) and Siena in 1974, a 'Music Digest' in London in 1977, three concerts in Paris in 1977 at the recently opened IRCAM Centre, six concerts at the Festival of Aix-en-Provence in 1979, a Ligeti evening in Budapest in 1979, a Ligeti Matinée in Munich and two concerts in Paris in 1981 in conjunction with the French première of *Le Grand Macabre*, a Ligeti evening in Vienna and a Ligeti Festival in Hall (Tyrol) also in 1981.

1

I

Várnai: First of all, I wonder if you could tell me which of all your works you consider the most important in your output. I ask this question because I should like to find a vantage point from which to view your stylistic development, looking at both your earlier and later works. You may not like to use the word development – I do not like it much either – so shall we say stylistic changes?

Ligeti: It is perhaps my Second Quartet which reflects my ideas most clearly – where you would find all the different techniques I have used. It was composed ten years ago, in 1968.

V.   What makes this work significant, in what way does it sum up your previous compositions and in what sense does it indicate what was to follow?

L.   To begin with, let me give you a resumé of the 'Ligeti style' through the transformations it has undergone. As you know, all my compositions dating back to Hungary show Bartók's influence very strongly, and to a lesser extent that of Stravinsky and of Berg's *Lyric Suite*. In the post-war years in Hungary we did not know much about other modern composers. Then, in the early '50s, I began to feel that I had to go beyond Bartók. It did not mean repudiating him, of course; stylistically, I have always maintained very strong links with him. What I felt I had to abandon were traditional forms, a musical language of the traditional kind, the sonata form. That gave me the impulse to 'break with Bartók'. I felt I had to adopt free compositional forms, like those you find in Debussy's late works, in *Jeux* or the Trio for flute, viola and harp. In these you find hardly any trace of formulating musical ideas in periodic form. I wanted to get away from all ready-made forms, which Bartók took seriously, and had learned from late Beethoven and from Liszt. Bartók's sonorities were still valid for me, also his chromaticism, but I had to get beyond formal structure as used by Bartók, and here I mean not

13

only the overall structural forms but also the small formal elements of a composition. Also, I had to get away from the idea of seeing music divided by bars altogether. Of course, I went on using bar-lines and conventional musical notation in most of my compositions; in the actual music, however, bar-lines had no other function for me than as points of reference, to keep the four string players of a quartet for instance from drifting away from one another. My music is a continuous flow, unbroken by bars, like a Gregorian melody. You could not analyse it according to Riemann's rules.

The thematic-motival structure and its role in the progress of music is almost completely abandoned. In this respect my Second Quartet sums up all my previous work. It also includes reminders of my Hungarian compositions, which show the influence of Bartók and Stravinsky. If you compare the First Quartet, composed in Hungary in 1953–54, with the Second, written fifteen years later in 1968, you can detect the sound of the First Quartet, a much dissolved manifestation of it, in the Second. Only the other day, I read a remark Ulrich Dibelius made about the Second Quartet; 'fahl, hektisch und verstiegen' (livid, hectic and freakish). You can find traces of these features in my early compositions, dating back to my Hungarian days. Already then I tended towards something irregular and freakish in music. Music should not be normal, well-bred, with its tie all neat. First in Cologne in 1957 and later during my long stay in Vienna in the '60s, I gradually evolved a musical style in which I abandoned structures conceived in terms of bars, melodies, lines and conventional forms. In this respect my first two orchestral works, *Apparitions* and *Atmosphères*, are the most radical. *Atmosphères* is just a floating, fluctuating sound, although it is polyphonic.

V.   That is what I wanted to ask in connection with what you said about having given up bar-lines and parts in your musical texture. For I do not think that is characteristic of *Atmosphères*.

L.   Technically speaking I have always approached musical texture through part-writing. Both *Atmosphères* and *Lontano* have a dense canonic structure. But you cannot actually hear the polyphony, the canon. You hear a kind of impenetrable texture, something like a very densely woven cobweb. I have retained melodic lines in the process of composition, they are governed by rules as strict as Palestrina's or those of the Flemish school, but the rules of this polyphony are worked out by me. The polyphonic structure does not actually come through, you cannot hear it; it remains hidden in a microscopic, under-water world, to us inaudible. I call it micropolyphony (such a beautiful word!). All in all, you cannot hear my music as it appears on paper. Of course, while actually composing each piece I worked on what we hear, as we hear it. The technical process of composition is like letting a crystal form in a supersaturated solution. The crystal is potentially there in the solution but becomes visible only at the moment of crystallization. In much the same way, you could say that there is a state of supersaturated polyphony, with all the 'crystal culture' in it but you cannot discern it. My aim was to arrest the process, to fix the supersaturated solution just at the moment before crystallization. Coming back to my Second Quartet, here I applied a similar process to chamber music. In orchestral works it was relatively easy, technically speaking, to create a dense polyphony; I had as many parts at my disposal as there were instruments in an orchestra. (That is why I broke down a string orchestra into individual instruments, although you cannot hear them as solo instruments.) In the case of a quartet, the problem was how to realize micropolyphony, a densely woven musical texture in the medium of chamber music. I had an example in my First Quartet, in which the last but one variation, just before the final section, is a kind of fugato, where the subject emerges from the fusion of two diatonic parts played by solo instruments. It is a chromatic subject. The two instrumental parts – two violins or a violoncello and a viola – are not fused but intertwine much more like twisted strands of a thread. Two diatonic solo parts combine to create a composite chromatic line, which is an idea characteristic of Bartók. That was my point of departure for 'woven' music like *Atmosphères*, where the inter-twined strands are so completely blended that you cannot discern the individual parts.

In the early '60s I was also interested in other areas of form and expression (in this case you cannot separate form from expression), in a frantic, tormented quality of sound which may seem like a disorderly, wild gesticulation, haphazard and completely uncontrolled. (German critics who analysed my work called it 'zerhackt'). At the same time I was really trying to find ways of transforming this 'superexpressiveness' into something cool, as if to put such wild musical gesticulating in a glass case, to see it as we see objects exhibited in a museum. As if a pane of glass or a supercooled sheet of ice separated us from the blazing heat of the

15

expression. You can find such wild gesticulating in my earlier works – *Aventures* and *Nouvelles Aventures* are the most typical examples – but the technique had not been fully developed until the Second Quartet.

Consequently, I could say that the Second Quartet is a synthesis, if only I did not dislike the word. There is everything in it: Bartók's initial influence, a tone of voice recalling Stravinsky and Alban Berg and all the characteristic features of my own music, the micropolyphony of *Atmosphères* and the cooled expressionism of *Aventures*. And also something else. I have always been fascinated by machines that do not work properly; in general, by the external world of technology and automation which engenders, and puts people at the mercy of, bureaucracies. Transposed into music, the ticking of malfunctioning machinery occurs in many of my works, including the Second Quartet.

V.   May I interrupt you at this point? It has always seemed to me that the machine-like, 'meccanico-type' movement, as a mode of expression, first appears around 1968, perhaps at the opening of *Continuum*. From what you have just said, am I to infer that the 'meccanico-type' was nothing new, it had always been there?

L.   No, not always. It was heralded by 'Horloges démoniaques', a short section of *Nouvelles Aventures*. And a still earlier manifestation of it is in *Poème symphonique* of 1962, written for 100 metronomes, which is the first pure example of meccanico music. But the composition of *Poème symphonique* was preceded by long years of reflection. Traces of it appear in the First Quartet, although no indications refer to it. One of the variations is a quite machine-like movement: a descending chromatic pizzicato of the violoncello and above it the viola and the second violin playing, mechanically, machine-like ornaments. Only the first violin pursues an independent, expressive melodic line. I can go even further back in time. I composed some such machine-like pieces for the piano as a schoolboy. I probably have the score somewhere. In one of them the left hand plays a mechanical progression of a tritone and the right hand something equally machine-like; two little machines at play. I composed a piece for four hands when I was eighteen or nineteen, before I knew Stravinsky's *Three Pieces for String Quartet*. In this work for four hands each part is an ostinato figure and the four ostinatos are superimposed rather as they are in Stravinsky.

Could I make a digression here and go outside the sphere of

music? In the works of Krudy[1] you find again and again a character, a widow whose husband was either a botanist or a meteorologist and has been dead for years. The widow lives alone in a house, mostly in Nyírség,[2] as Krudy's characters often do, and, another typical feature, she is quite isolated. She would have a house among the dunes which is full of clocks, barometers, hygrometers. I don't know if you can remember this figure, who appears in several of his works and is the subject of one of his short stories. I was a child, I must have been about five, when I came upon a volume of Krudy's short stories, which was a book quite unsuitable for children; someone gave it to me by mistake. It was in summer and I remember being overcome by a strange melancholy, perhaps because of the heat, or was it my reading these Krudy stories all alone in the loft? One of the stories was about the widow living in a house full of clocks ticking away all the time. The meccanico-type music really originates from reading that story as a five-year-old, on a hot summer afternoon. Afterwards, other everyday experiences came to be added to the memory of the house full of ticking clocks; images of buttons we push and a machine would start working or not, as the case may be, lifts that sometimes work and sometimes do not, or stop at the wrong floor; the Chaplin film, *Modern Times*, one of the great movie experiences of my childhood. Recalcitrant machinery, unmanageable automata have always fascinated me.

V.   All that is in the quartet?

L.   Yes, all that and a lot more.

V.   Well perhaps we could, after all, use the word synthesis.

L.   Yes, perhaps. The Second Quartet sums up all the different kinds of music I had composed, all the various technical and expressive features, the floating quality of *Atmosphères*, the machine-like character of my composition for 100 metronomes, the cooled expressionism of *Aventures*. But do not misunderstand me, I do not mean that the Second Quartet is my most important work.

V.   The purpose of my first question was to find a point of reference. Before going on to the next questions could we return to something you have referred to several times, and go into it in

---

[1] Krudy, Gyula (1878–1933). Hungarian novelist and man of letters. A great stylist. In his nostalgic dreamworld of pre-World War I Hungary his finely drawn characters are often portrayed with both cool irony and profound sympathy (tr.)

[2] A sandy region in north-east Hungary (tr.)

greater detail? You have dwelt with particular emphasis on a certain 'cooled expressionism'. Would you tell me more exactly what it means? I find the very concept self-contradictory: deep-frozen expressionism.

L.   There are two aspects to it, one stylistic, a matter peculiar to our generation, and the other a matter of personal taste. People of my generation, who are now around fifty, like myself, found in our younger days anything romantic and especially anything sentimental very alien to us, anything syrupy, smacking of Puccini or, say, of Lehár. Our ideals ranged somewhere between Mozart and Bartók. As we saw it, there was the age of the Baroque, then Classical music up to Mozart; the period following that was 'suspect' but was superseded by another period of 'character and integrity': Bartók and Stravinsky. That is not how I feel today, of course, the range of my taste is much wider. I accept nineteenth-century music, very much so; Schumann is one of my favourite composers (which reminds me, the overwrought, hectic character of my Second Quartet shows Schumann's influence on me). The Mahler revival, the cult of art nouveau, we see all that in a quite different light nowadays. You need not reject everything just because it is fashionable. Taste is being revised all the time, works are re-valued or de-valued. Just think that for our fathers' generation Bosch or Brueghel were mere curiosities.

V.   If they knew them at all.

L.   In late nineteenth-century editions of Baedeker you look in vain for Brueghel's pictures of Vienna or Bosch's paintings in Madrid. Renaissance harmony was the ideal of that generation. Just as Bosch and Brueghel came to be reassessed and Mannerism rediscovered by the middle of the twentieth century, in the last fifteen to twenty years Romanticism, and especially Romantic music, has been re-evaluated. Musicians have come to realise that the cult of Classicism is nothing more than a narrow conformism of taste, a mere fashion. Going back to the cooled expressionism of my own music, I want to remove great, whirling passions, all grand expressive gestures, far away and view them at a distance. My generation's old attitude comes into play here, a rejection of pathos and romanticism. I was brought up in an atmosphere when this was the prevailing taste in the arts, and although I now accept Romanticism, *in my music* I remain true to my upbringing. I do not like open, unmitigated expressionism, like pictures of Schmidt-Rotluff, Kirchner or Kokoschka, and the German expressionist school in general.

18

V.   What about music?

L.   I respect Schoenberg's expressionism in *Erwartung*, for instance, but it is just as alien to me as *Pierrot Lunaire*.

V.   That is not exactly what I wanted to know. I should really like you to explain how in music and by musical means you can hope to realize a 'distancing', a 'cooled' quality. Perhaps I should tell you what makes me ask that. When I listen to the *Dies irae* in your Requiem, which reveals on the whole the same 'gesticulating' musical material and treatment, I find that I cannot help taking it seriously.

L.   It is a serious piece.

V.   Where is the coolness then, the deep-frozen quality?

L.   The Requiem actually is a very good example. The *Dies irae* sequence in the text has always interested me, it has exercised my mind ever since my youth; it is an extraordinarily colourful, almost comic-strip, representation of the Last Judgement. I find it particularly fascinating that the poet resorted to colourfulness to resolve fear. Although neither of us likes the word alienation, here it is very apt, also with reference to the text. Characteristically, I stopped at *Lacrimosa*. The work starts with *Introitus*, goes on with *Kyrie* and ends with *Dies irae*; *Dies irae* is pivotal in the Requiem. There is all my own fear in it, my real life experiences, a lot of terrifying childhood fantasies, and yet the music resolves all that as well. As if to say, we do not have to live in fear; or you could put it like this, we are certainly going to die but so long as we are alive we believe that we shall live for ever. (That is also the subject of my opera.) Now I come back to what I mean by deep-frozen expressionism. Overwrought musical gestures result in turning the screw beyond the limit set for it. I deprive both pathos and expression of credibility, suddenly everything gets out of gear. I could say such music is somehow mad (I do not mean in the psychological sense of the word); it is mad because it overflows the banks, changes its course – not that it had any noticeable course. If pathos in a gesture is excessive you can no longer perceive or register it.

V.   That is what I wanted to find out. So you think that by overdoing something you make it lose credibility and you turn it into its opposite.

L.   No, it does not go that far. As an example let me turn to Webern, who has been the model for many composers. His treatment of melodic lines, his wide intervals are typical of what we call super-expressionism. Think of the canons or the songs of his middle period; they are so overcharged that in effect they turn completely cold. It all evolved eventually into Webern's late style, which is crystalline and deep-frozen. A late Webern is almost like Calder's wire mobiles. Webern has undoubtedly influenced my music, in the *Dies irae* of the Requiem most of all. But it was not a decisive influence, I was brushed by him, no more; I am not a follower. To be specific, I should say that such expressionism is so overstrained that it can no longer be seen as expression, it turns into a statue of itself. With Webern it does not become comical as partly happens in *Le Grand Macabre*, where the very subject of the opera lends itself to such treatment; yet, in the opera what is comical is at the same time demoniac, just as in the earlier *Aventures*. Listening to *Aventures* for the first time, you at once become aware of its funny side. Later, when you have heard it several times and are familiar with the music, you may come to find it terrifying. But at no stage can you regard it as expressionist in the sense that Schoenberg's music is; it is certainly not filled with pathos.

V. Two questions arise from what you have just said. First of all, I tend to ask composers what they think is the relationship between their life and their work, or in other words where do they draw their inspiration from?

L. Do you mean actual experiences?

V. Yes, whether your life influences your creative work.

L. It certainly does.

V. What I am driving at is whether an event, an experience can trigger off a work, or is the source of inspiration purely musical?

L. I think you can look at it in two ways. Every individual has personal experience as well as collective experiences which he shares with a community or a nation. There is no doubt that both influence one's work. But experience in itself is not enough. To take a slightly forced analogy, you could see art, artistic creation, as a soup constantly simmering in a cauldron. The taste of the soup depends on what you have put in it; the broth simmering over the fire is the artist's potential and what you put into it are the experiences. Creative activity in music, painting or literature is not directly prompted by an experience you have just been through. You have to look for it in your genes or in childhood experiences. There are a number of people of great potential talent and some of them become creative artists while others become bookkeepers. And you cannot overlook social circumstances either – some talented people do not turn into artists because they have to earn their living as upholsterers. But then there have been upholsterers who became great painters.

There is no doubt that external circumstances, both personal and shared experiences, everything that happens around an artist, social and economic circumstances, wars, technical developments, cultural surroundings and his own general attitude to life leave their mark on a picture, a piece of music, a novel. But for the picture, the piece of music or novel to take actual shape you need an individual creative will, an artist's talent. The external world does not affect this inner core of creativity. In my case to come back to the Requiem and *Le Grand Macabre*, one dimension of my music bears the imprint of a long time spent in the shadow of death both as an individual and as the member of a group. Not that it lends a tragic quality to my music, quite the opposite. Anyone who has been through horrifying experiences is not likely to create terrifying works of art in all seriousness. He is more likely to alienate . . .

V. Or go to the other extreme.

L. I am not walking along a plank which is just about to give way, whistling as I go. That is not my style.

V. Which makes me think of Mozart, the perfect harmony of his last period, when he was in worse circumstances than ever.

L. That is exactly what I mean; if you try to understand a work from the actual circumstances of the artist, you will get nowhere. It is a rather childish idea that a composer will write music in the minor key when he is sad, it is rather too simplistic. There is no doubt, however, that the stance of the artist, his whole approach to his art, his means of expression are all of them greatly influenced by experiences he has accumulated in the course of day-to-day living.

V. An artistic personality is formed by an artist's experiences added to his genetic inheritance. Shall we apply this to a particular work, taking for instance *Continuum*? The immediate reason for writing it was that you were commissioned by the Swiss harpsichord player, Antoinette Vischer. But how did it come to be the kind of music it is?

L. I can quite clearly remember the circumstances. An event can prompt you; if someone commissions me to write a piece of music or asks me to do it, well, that is important. Also composers have to make a living. If I have the work in me potentially, such an event could – as I usually put it – sound the bell in me. That is the level where external incentives operate. We know, for instance, that Bach's motets, which are among his best music, were always commissioned for funerals and that works commissioned for funerals were always very well paid. But whether music composed in such circumstances is going to be good or bad, that is quite another matter.

If an event does not manage to sound the bell in me, nothing happens. When I was living in very strained circumstances in the early '60s, someone asked me to compose a choral work with organ accompaniment. I refused. I *can* write music for organ and also have ideas for choral works but the two together conjured up in me Liszt's choral works with organ accompaniment and suddenly my enthusiasm was gone, I did not feel like doing it. Sometimes it is just the opposite. A few weeks ago a pianist from Hamburg asked me to write a trio for violin, piano and horn. He, an excellent hornplayer, and a violinist had formed a trio but were reduced to playing nothing but Brahms's Horn Trio, for there are no other chamber works for these three instruments. I agreed straight away. As soon as he pronounced the word horn, somewhere inside my head I heard the sound of a horn as if coming from a distant forest in a fairy tale, just as in a poem by Eichendorff. Much the same happened with *Continuum*. It had never occurred to me before to write for the harpsichord, but as soon as I had read Antoinette Vischer's letter it suddenly came to me that a harpsichord was really like some strange machine – at the time I was rather interested in models of machines. I also remembered that a harpsichord was most typically an instrument with a non-continuous sound, the twang of the string is of short duration, followed by silence. I thought to myself, what about composing a piece of music that would be a paradoxically continuous sound, something like *Atmosphères*, but that would have to consist of innumerable thin slices of salami? A harpsichord has an easy touch; it can be played very fast, almost fast enough to reach the level of continuum, but not quite (it takes about eighteen separate sounds per second to reach the threshold where you can no longer make out individual notes and the limit set by the mechanism of the harpsichord is about fifteen to sixteen notes a second). As the string is plucked by the plectrum, apart from the tone you also hear quite a loud noise. The entire process is a series of sound impulses in rapid succession which create the impression of continuous sound. As soon as I had read the letter I knew what kind of music I would write, it all arose from the sound quality of the harpsichord.

Perhaps I should also mention here that in music for the keyboard my models are Scarlatti, Chopin and Schumann. I do not mean that other composers did not write marvellous piano music but these three composers' musical ideas arose essentially from the piano, from the characteristics of the instrument, from what our ten fingers can do. They provide the best example of music completely adapted to the sound quality of an instrument. Or think of the orchestral sound in Stravinsky's works. With Reger or Hindemith a melody is all the same whether it is played, for example, on the flute or on the clarinet. But when Stravinsky wrote a tune for the clarinet he made use of the specific acoustic properties of the clarinet with regard to the partials. That is also my idea: to take into account the specific properties of every instrument and of the human voice in composing music. When the sound of an instrument or a group of instruments or the human voice finds an echo in me, in the musical idea within me, then I can sit down and compose, otherwise I cannot. For instance, if someone asked me now to write a work for the orchestra I should refuse, since I am at the moment interested in other things.

V. In the case of the commission for *Continuum* there was a happy coincidence of being commissioned to write a piece for a particular instrument with an idea maturing in you about a machine-like, meccanico-type music.

L. I have often been asked how I feel about being commissioned to compose music. Well, it is of course nice to be paid for music you write. So long as money remains a means of transactions, so long as you can buy food, pay for a home and other pleasant things in life with money, a composer is as much in need of it as an upholsterer or assistant bookkeeper. The prospect of earning money by itself is not enough to strike a resonance in the artist, but it may well increase his enthusiasm – think of Bach's motets that we mentioned earlier. We need have no illusions about that.

V. Has it ever happened to you that the prospect of financial reward meant more than the sounding of your inner bell?

L. No, it never has. Not even at the time I had very little money, between 1956 and the mid-sixties. Being a well-known composer, as I have been since *Apparitions*, does not necessarily mean that you are well paid. The few performances of my works did not bring in much, I was reduced to a Bohemian, almost 'clochard' existence. Yet I refused to write film music, even in those days, although it would have been very lucrative. I was afraid that it would compromise my talent. I wanted to be radical and not to compromise my ideas. This may sound pompous but that was the aim I set myself in life. When, in the early '60s, I could have had the opportunity to write film music without any stylistic preconditions I still refused. I did not wish to get into the world of cinema, I had the feeling it was a world that would corrupt you. The first commission for film music is soon followed by the next. You quickly get used to the idea of what mood is required for a particular sequence, you are influenced by the knowledge of what atmosphere is wanted as background for particular scenes, you compose with a stop-watch, minding the seconds: all that has a corrupting effect. I do not think that Mozart would have been able to write his quartets dedicated to Haydn if he had composed film music earlier.

V. I could mention a counter-example. Honegger made a living from writing film music without compromising his talent; he was able to write his important works. In this respect our opinion about his important works is immaterial.

L. Honegger is indeed a good example. He was one of the best people working for the cinema industry. But 'applied art' somehow, somewhere, compromised his attitude, his creative personality suffered, his compositions were affected by it. That is why he never reached the standard of Bartók or Stravinsky. Although Stravinsky weakens my case; he wrote *Circus Polka*. I do not wish to object to seizing an opportunity, what I mean is simply that money, the world of cinema may have a corrupting influence. I was exposed to this risk but I was able to say no. I preferred walking instead of riding on the tram to compromising myself. You may find this rather grand of me, but that is how it was.

V. My next question is a bit tricky. Erkki Salmenhaara said in his analysis of your music that a dualistic view of the world comes through in your works. Do you think he is right? Would you say that either the 'static' music of *Atmosphères* or your wildly gesticulating overstrained style has anything to do with your childhood experiences? In the programme notes to the first performance of *Atmosphères* you write about a childhood dream;[3] has that dream played a decisive role in your music?

24

L.   I do not think that we should overestimate the importance of childhood experiences, they do not determine all future events. Nobody knows of course which aspects of his character or which events in his life are consequences of some event in his childhood, what adult idiosyncrasies or interests have their roots in early life. Let me give an example which patently has nothing to do with my childhood. In the past few years I have been very interested in the music of Charles Ives, which you could see as a musical process resulting from the random superimposition of several independent layers. I never heard anything like that as a child. We know, however, that Ives's father, who was a military band-leader, on one occasion arranged for three brass bands to march towards the main square of their village. They came from three different directions, each playing a different march. That was the first time Ives had heard three different marches played simultaneously. We also know that Mahler was a keen observer of how the sound of various brass bands, roundabouts and musical automata blended at a fair; he thought that was real polyphony. And it is what you find in the development section of his Third Symphony.

I really do not know how important such musical or other experiences are. I have never given much thought to it. I only brought up that particular childhood dream in connection with

---

[3] As a small child I once had a dream that I could not get to my cot, to my safe haven, because the whole room was filled with a dense confused tangle of fine filaments. It looked like the web I had seen silkworms fill their box with as they change into pupas. I was caught up in this immense web together with both living things and objects of various kinds – huge moths, a variety of beetles – which tried to get to the flickering flame of the candle in the room; enormous dirty pillows were suspended in this substance, their rotten stuffing hanging out through the slits in the torn covers. There were blobs of fresh mucus, balls of dry mucus, remnants of food all gone cold and other such revolting rubbish. Every time a beetle or a moth moved, the entire web started shaking so that the big, heavy pillows were swinging about, which, in turn, made the web rock harder. Sometimes the different kinds of movement reinforced one another and the shaking became so hard that the web tore in places and a few insects suddenly found themselves free. But their freedom was short-lived, they were soon caught up again in the rocking tangle of filaments, and their buzzing, loud at first, grew weaker and weaker. The succession of these sudden, unexpected events gradually brought about a change in the internal structure, in the texture of the web. In places knots formed, thickening into an almost solid mass, caverns opened up where shreds of the original web were floating about like gossamer. All these changes seemed like an irreversible process, never returning to earlier states again. An indescribable sadness hung over these shifting forms and structure, the hopelessness of passing time and the melancholy of unalterable past events.

Apparitions – it is just one of all those hundreds of dreams that I can no longer remember – because, working on *Apparitions*, I tried for the first time to create an impenetrable texture of sound, a dense mass of oversaturated polyphony. The idea of an impenetrable texture of sound evoked immediate associations, cobwebs, silkworms, etc. Here my fear of spiders also comes into it, it is not just a childhood memory but a phobia that is still with me. When I was three years old I stayed with my aunt at Csikszereda[4] for three months, as construction work was going on at our house. She was a teacher at an elementary school and had the idea that children had to overcome their aversions. When she realised that I was afraid of spiders she made me collect cobwebs with bare hands. It terrified and disgusted me. Whether this explains my dream about the cobwebs and the impenetrable web of sound, an original Ligeti invention, I cannot tell. My arachnophobia may have contributed to it. But I think it would be rather naïve to say that composing such music was a way of working this fear of spiders out of my system.

My counterpoint studies under Veress and Farkas certainly played an important role in working out impenetrable textures of sound, as did studying Jeppesen, which Kodály made *de rigueur* for would-be composers. My keen interest in the Flemish composers, in Ockeghem in particular, was also a contributing factor. To this day, I am more interested in Ockeghem than in Palestrina, because his music does not tend towards culminating points. Just as one voice approaches a climax another voice comes to counteract it, like waves in the sea. The unceasing continuity of Ockeghem's music, a progress without development, was one point of departure for me to think in terms of impenetrable textures of sound. Also what I learned at the electronic studios in Cologne, the superimposed layers of re-corded sound, played its part. You will find that, even though indirectly, such techniques affected my musical language, the orchestral polyphony of *Atmosphères* and *Apparitions*.

A whole range of experiences find their way into music, all that we assimilate both emotionally and all the technical skills we acquire are factors that shape a composer's music. Childhood experiences play their part, of course. For instance I like opera as a genre very much. We moved to Kolozsvár[5] when I was six, and there, as a seven-year-old, I was first taken to the opera. The

[4] A small town in South-East Transylvania
[5] The largest town and cultural centre of Transylvania

26

most frequent performances were of Verdi, Bizet, Rossini and *Boris Godunov*; Mozart was heard much less; Wagner not at all. In *Le Grand Macabre* you can find various types of musical gestures that are derived from my early favourites. Verdi of the middle period and *Carmen* had simply been built into me, I do not have to think about them to try to recall them, they are always there in me.

V. So you think that those who define your music as presenting a dualistic view of the world are wrong? The contrast between the static, impenetrable textures on the one hand and the wildly gesticulating yet deep-frozen expressionism on the other is not an essential feature?

L. You could say that only if I had died in 1965 and my early compositions, dating back to Hungary, had been lost. But taking both the early works and those written since 1965, it would not be correct to hold such a view.

V. As I consider our conversation a kind of general introduction, perhaps I may change the subject and go on with an entirely different kind of question. I do not know if I am right but I have noticed in your Cello Concerto – which in my view is a very significant work, particularly seen in the whole context of contemporary music – something I had never heard before. I mean the rediscovery of the octave. Contemporary composers in general abhor the octave, whereas since the Cello Concerto it has practically become one of the distinctive features of your musical style. What made you use octaves?

L. My general attitude not only in music but in all other areas of life is not to take anything for granted. When something is asserted and it sounds good my immediate reaction is to go below the surface to see what reality I find there. Slick phrases, attractive philosophical systems tend to leave me cold. Schoenberg's twelve-note system is such an attractive dogma, it eliminates the octave. According to Schoenberg reinforcing a note in the octave makes it too weighty; a duplicated note gives the impression that it is returning too early in the series of pitches. (In the music of Webern, who was more strictly consistent than Schoenberg, when several series intersect on a note it is always in unison, not in the octave). The Vienna serialists had a horror of major thirds, perfect fifths, of major and minor chords, of diminished sevenths. The reason for their aversion was that they felt these intervals had been worn out, depleted. From a stylistic point of view that is quite understandable. (I also tend to shun old, worn-out musical techniques, so what I say about the serialists would also apply to me. There are tunes and rhythmic patterns in *Apparitions*, but they are deliberately faded, their outlines blurred. I felt then that melody, harmony and rhythm could no longer be used as formal elements in the musical process.) Serialists, Boulez in particular, observe the rule of shunning octaves. But what is that all about, I asked myself at one point; since I do not write twelve-note music, is it sensible for me to avoid octaves?

V. Yet octaves do not appear in your music until a particular point.

L. Would you say that I avoided octaves before the Cello Concerto?

V. In any case that was where I first noticed them used deliberately, as a special mark of your musical style.

L. You mean at the end of the first movement, when the deep notes of the double-bass just for one moment double the harmonics of the cello at the octave? I should say that the purpose of that was rather to delineate the lower and upper limits of a vast, empty space. I did not deliberately set out to return to the use of octaves.

V. You would definitely say that my observation is not correct?

L. Well, no, I am only saying that I had used octaves as well as other intervals earlier too. I reject the twelve-note dogma of shunning octaves even if I make use of the full chromatic scale and avoid tonal centres.

V. Here I have to disagree with what you are saying. From the Cello Concerto or perhaps the *Lacrimosa* of your Requiem onwards octaves appear in your works, octaves and other perfect intervals, the fifth, the tritone; perfect intervals in accented positions are quite definitely a characteristic of your style.

L. You mean that certain intervals appear at certain points, signalling junctures of form? In *Lontano*, for instance, a C is reinforced across several octaves to mark the end of the first formal unit. But you may well be right about two intervals. I have also noticed how often I used octaves and tritones (augmented fourths) in marking off sections of formal structures. The sound gets gradually crystallised and, on reaching an octave or a tritone, it comes to a sudden halt to go on again a moment later. But my 'markers' are not based on theoretical considerations or dogmas. Other intervals also assume a dominant position. In *Continuum*, for instance, at one point you can hear nothing but a minor third,

28

at another point a minor third plus a major second. At junctures of form you would rarely find a major third or a fifth, since – and you may call that dogmatic – I do shun major triads. And I have yet another 'dogmatic aversion' of that kind; as far as possible, I avoid Webernian major sevenths and diminished ninths, made up of a tritone and a fourth or fifth; for me these have the connotation diminished sevenths had for Schoenberg: worn, depleted. Hence my preference for two-pole, empty tritones, octaves, major seconds or indeed two major seconds on top of one another. And another 'typical Ligeti signal' is a fourth made up of a minor third and a major second or the other way round. (*Lux aeterna* and *Lontano* are based on that.)

V. The reason I have raised this question was not the striking purity of the octaves. I think it is a much more important stylistic feature than just that. I wonder if you'll agree or disagree with what I am going to say. I have noticed in the last seven to eight years or so that some traditional features have been appearing in one way or another, and with increasing frequency, in the works of major contemporary composers: the octave, classical forms, music of descriptive power, a fully developed melody line, periodic rhythm. What I want to ask you is this: do you now also feel tied to our classical tradition and if so do you think it is a logical consequence of your development?

L. In the period of the most extravagant experimentation, in the Darmstadt of the late '50s, I was considered a particularly traditionalist composer. Now in our much more conformist times, when many composers are harking back to neo-romanticism and tonality, I appear very experimental. I do not think I am much influenced by prevailing fashions. Not that I remain completely unaffected by them. But it never occurred to me, for instance, to join the 'official' serialists of Darmstadt-Cologne. I dislike the idea of being a member of a clique.

You can observe a certain alternation of fashions in the history of music, in which a more experimentally-minded period is followed by one leaning more towards tradition. I do not speak of fashion in a derogatory sense, I simply mean trends. Machaut and Landini started something genuinely new, which was very experimental. The Flemish school then developed it into some form of classical style. Also, Monteverdi's seconda prattica represented an immensely bold step when it first appeared, but had turned into old-fashioned, stuffy conformism by the time of Bach's sons. In my opinion the time for new, decisive innovations always comes when a particular musical tradition has run out of steam. Just think of Debussy coming after Saint-Saëns and Fauré. There are periods when the renewal of musical language is of little consequence. There is not much new in Mozart's musical language compared to the novelty of the Mannheim school and of J.C. Bach. Mozart created something outstandingly new but not in the technical aspects of musical language. I think that a change in style is brought on partly by the potentiality inherent in the music of a period and partly by a transformation of the general cultural context. In Central Europe after the collapse of Nazism there was a cultural vacuum, which was filled by Stravinsky, Hindemith, Schoenberg and Webern. Then a number of composers, bursting with new ideas, happened to come together in Darmstadt. It had to be in Germany, where the cultural vacuum was most pronounced; Germany after all was in the eye of the storm. All that has changed by now. There has now been a period of ten years marked by some form of consolidation, of the wrong kind, I should say. In many areas I have become aware of a marked trend back to romanticism. Some people call it nostalgia, the French say 'retro'; it has become chic, it is all the rage. We can never tell what will ultimately come from a fashion – the Mannheim style was also a fashion in its time. As far as I am concerned I did not follow Stockhausen or Cage when they were the guiding stars but went on in my own way. Now we find nostalgia in the same dominant position and again I do not follow this trend either but remain independent. I seem to have some built-in stabilizing force. I am, of course, influenced by everything that is happening today in music, literature, painting and in the world in general, but I am not overpowered by it; I seem to be weighted so as to stand upright again, however much I am rocked.

You ask me how far I am tied to tradition. While I was working out micropolyphony – in the period of *Apparitions* and *Atmosphères* – I never for a moment lost sight of my models of the past. I mentioned Ockeghem and Flemish polyphony as evidence. But the kind of reversion I can now observe in the twenty- to thirty-year-olds of even mature gifts is not for me. In the late '50s and early '60s my music moved within harmonic fields filled out with chromaticism, whereas ten years later I composed diatonic and microtonal music. I felt that chromaticism had been exhausted: the choice was between going 'back' to diatonic music and going 'forward' outside the sphere of tempered music. Tradition and experimentation are both there side by side.

V. Is that the reason why polyphony as you employed it in *Atmosphères* – a combination of parts restricted to a very narrow range – becomes, in *Melodien*, an equally dense polyphony, where the parts follow bold, wide-ranging melodic lines?

L. That is so. Hence the programmatic title, *Melodien*.

V. Can it conceivably happen that a quite openly 'cantabile' melodic quality comes through the dense polyphonic texture?

L. Take *Le Grand Macabre*. That is a case in point, although of course opera as a genre makes tunes practically inevitable. Not necessarily tunes as in Mozart or Verdi, because I somehow feel ashamed to write tuneful melodies quite openly.

V. Are you really so shy about it?

L. Yes, although not without a degree of exhibitionism. I am really not as shy as all that.

To sum up the stylistic changes my music has gone through, first of all I should say that whenever I feel that certain melodic or rhythmic models or formal structures have gone stale, I switch my interest to some other area, but my basic approach remains unchanged. What did actually happen? Having gone through *Apparitions*, *Atmosphères*, the *Kyrie* of the Requiem, I felt that total chromaticism, the world of filled clusters had ceased to have any more interest for me. If I went on composing that type of music it would simply be an imitation of my earlier work, I would just be chewing the cud. So I switched my technical interest to an area where I could still produce something new. Gradually the 'interval signals' emerged; the octave, which in such a stark form would have been impossible in *Atmosphères*. These interval signals were neither tonal nor atonal yet somehow, with their purity and clarity they constituted points of rest, they afforded the possibility of operating with alternate tension and resolution. Then gradually this type of music grew stale, which drove me outside the sphere of equal temperament. The question was what I could do with various kinds of microtonal intervals – I do not mean quarter-tones, which are simply semitones divided by two. I could point to examples of microtonality in *Ramifications*, the Double Concerto, the second movement of the Second Quartet. But my opera is back in the world of equal temperament – micro-intervals are for chamber ensembles or soloists. In the rougher medium of an opera or a symphony orchestra micro-intervals would simply produce 'smudginess'. Diatonic, chromatic and tonal music having been exhausted I had to find another area to work on, with more scope. I tend to want to do something new, if possible. I am not after novelty for its own sake, I do not want to assume absurd postures, but if something has already been it is ready, complete, gone and done with.

V. Does that apply just to yourself or do you see it as a principle that applies generally?

L. Since today there is no accepted norm in musical language everybody must find his own. We are forced to look for something new, which puts me right at the opposite pole from nostalgia or neo-tonality. I feel that to revert to the great tradition of the past is tantamount to taking refuge in 'safe' music. There is another way of continuing the work of the great masters of the past, composing at the same level as represented, say, by the late Beethoven sonatas, but in a new language, a new style. There is a task for you! Going back to the same musical idiom will not do.

V. Your principle is to keep looking for new material, new means once the old medium and techniques have been exhausted. Is there a point where you can stop this search?

L. No I do not think there is. In the Piano Concerto I am working on at the moment I use equal tempered chromaticism and I am trying to find rhythmic combinations which have not yet gone stale.

I should welcome a generally accepted musical language, such as tonality used to be. In the context of tonality it was of an extraordinary interest when Liszt invented a new modulation, which no one had ever heard before. Since we now have no universal language such events are no longer imaginable. Serialism, which Boulez had thought would gain universal currency, turned out to be a mere episode in musical history. During the three hundred years of the rule of tonality, dialects of the generally accepted musical language could be tolerated. Twelve-note music and serial music are synthetic constructions, incapable of organic change. Comparing a town where Renaissance and Baroque buildings were added to a medieval nucleus with a new town designed in an architectural office I find that spontaneously, organically developed towns have more vitality, a greater capacity to survive.

V. I come back to the same question: do you think that eventually the whole medium of sound will be exhausted and no new ways left?

L. There is an infinite number of possibilities.

II

V. In our conversation yesterday we tried to give a general outline of your musical style. We spoke about the different stages of your development, of your compositional ideas and principles and of other matters musical and outside the sphere of music. Today let us proceed by examining your output chronologically and in greater detail. A review like that should possibly start with the period 'before birth'. I think that the works in which your mature style, the real Ligeti sound, first appear are *Apparitions* and *Atmosphères*, although some early indication can be found in your pieces composed in Budapest.

In what has been written about you, the same remark appears again and again and you yourself have said the same thing when speaking about your music, namely that you did not even try to realize compositional ideas found in *Atmosphères* and *Apparitions* while you were living in Hungary. I am not referring to the utter impossibility of getting such works performed in the '50s but rather asking why you thought it impossible even to entertain such plans as were later realised in *Atmosphères* and *Apparitions*. Why did you not compose music just for yourself without giving any thought about getting it performed?

L. I first began to think about a kind of static music you find in *Atmosphères* and *Apparitions* in 1950; music wholly enclosed within itself, free of tunes, in which there are separate parts but they are not discernable, music that would change through gradual transformation almost as if it changed its colour from the inside. Before writing down a composition, first I always imagine what it would sound like; I can practically hear the various instruments play. Around 1950, I could *hear* the music I imagined but I did not possess the *technique* of imagining it put on paper. The main trouble was that the possibility had never occurred to me to write music without bars and bar-lines. Whereas I would have been able to note down the harmonic structures and clusters I had in mind I was stuck when it came to the notation of metre and rhythm. I did not know what time signatures to use. The first time I had an inkling of such a possibility was when – later on in Cologne – I heard of space notation, in which there are no bars, only a time-scale given, for instance, in seconds. Up till then I had not got beyond the concept of notation based on metre; I was still very much under the influence of Bartók and Stravinsky.

V. Do you mean that the whole problem was simply a notational difficulty? Yesterday you were talking about plain-chant; there are no bars in plain-chant either.

L. Quite so, but I did not think of noting down an orchestral work all in neumes without putting a metrical grid over it. It was both a notational and a compositional difficulty. *Musica ricercata* and *Métamorphoses nocturnes* are divided up into bars, they are conceived within the framework of conventional time measurement and periodic structure. Yes, it was more than a problem of notation. The change in my musical style did not really coincide with my leaving Hungary. My first 'static' piece dates back to the summer of 1956. And anyway you find the same kind of music in the Prelude to *Rheingold* and in *The Wooden Prince*. I did not realise that until later. There was a lot of information and knowledge I still had to acquire. The most important thing I did in Cologne was to listen to all the new music composed in the early '50s, of which I had previously had very little idea. The result was an improvement in my technique of composition.

V. How did listening to new music help, since nobody wrote static music at the time?

L. That is true, but I heard Schoenberg's *Five Pieces for Orchestra*, its *Farben* movement and became aware of the connection with *Rheingold* and *The Wooden Prince*. In addition, I went through a period when my compositional technique matured considerably.

What I learned in Cologne came as a shock; that was the first time I set eyes on a Boulez score and Stockhausen was then working on *Gruppen*, which is scored for three orchestras. There certainly was something in the general atmosphere which warranted the feeling of the Cologne group that they were creating something radically new. The most important members of the group were Stockhausen and Gottfried Michael Koenig. Stockhausen was extremely kind to me, I stayed at his house for six weeks; but he was already up in the clouds, he considered himself the world's greatest composer. Mauricio Kagel got to Cologne at about the same time as me. As far as technical knowledge was concerned I learned most from Koenig.

V. You arrived in Cologne with the idea of a certain 'static music'; then came all the new impressions, a sudden shock, technical studies. What attracted you to electronic music, a field so different from what you were planning on arriving in Cologne?

34

L. I had become interested in electronic music much earlier. I heard about it in a radio programme in 1953; I did not hear the music, I only heard *about* it. The programme said that all possible musical ideas could be realized in an electronic studio, which I fully believed, although now I do not think it is the case. It all sounded very logical. Music is freed from the shackles of instruments, any sound can be synthetically produced from pure sine waves. It fired my imagination and I absolutely wanted to go to Cologne. (That was one of the reasons for my leaving Hungary in December 1956.) On reaching Vienna, I got in touch with the Cologne studio and was given a scholarship to go there in early 1957. The scholarship was for just four months but it took me about six months to acquire the technical knowledge necessary for working in the studio. In those days I thought it was up to us composers to realize all our ideas in the studio. With experience these optimistic ideas were gradually reduced to a more realistic level. It turned out that whilst in theory you can synthesize sine waves into any kind of sound and produce any timbre or complex chord, time is a limiting factor. When you sound an oboe you have the whole spectrum of sound straight away. You can piece together such a sound by recording each element, all the harmonics on tape and then splice the synchronized sound together. But it is such a laborious process that a few seconds of the entire complex range of harmonics of the oboe sound take a year or two to produce – well I exaggerate a little. So think of the real synthetic sound, the creation of a completely new sound texture that you want to bring forth, that is a much more difficult task; and it is not just a question of time. It takes a year before you actually hear what you have imagined and by then your ideas will almost certainly have changed quite radically. (This applies only to those early days. Nowadays there are computers in electronic studios and such technical work can be completed in a matter of seconds.)

V. That was the reason why after having produced an electronic piece and drawn up plans for another you abandoned the medium for good?

L. That was not the only reason. Working in the studio gave me quite new compositional ideas, new factors had come to influence my development. While I was there I made a detailed analysis of Boulez's *Structures Ia*, with the result that whilst I found serial music extremely interesting I realised that it was not for me. I was fascinated by serialism but found it too dogmatic. And, as I said

35

earlier, I detest dogmas. Looking at the historical development of serialism what do we see? Within our system of temperament there emerged slowly a sound structure based on twelve notes. Schoenberg's twelve-note system was the logical continuation of what had been known since *Tristan*, i.e. that every note can be both tonic and leading note, which means that all notes are equal. Webern's method was to divide the twelve-note series into cells of three or four notes and work within a crystal-structure system of this kind. The result was an extremely homogeneous and consistent musical style. Following Messiaen's initiative, the next step was made by Goyvaerts, Boulez and Stockhausen in the early '50s. Since there is a twelve-note system, there should also be twelve different note lengths, twelve grades of dynamic intensity, etc. I said to myself, there may be a good reason for the number twelve as far as pitch is concerned; that is done by the tempered scale. But why take twelve grades of dynamic intensity? There could just as well be five or twenty. Moreover, a C sharp is what it is, a D is a D; they are exactly defined. But the difference between mezzoforte, forte and più forte is very subjective. The same applies to time measurement. What really interested me was flexible rhythm, giving up the pulsating metrical idiom. I had the chance of listening to Messiaen's works while staying in Cologne, and was most impressed by the entirely new and interesting rhythmic configuration in his music. Messiaen would choose a number of different time-measurements and arrange them in sequence with the result that metrical pulsation disappears and a floating kind of music takes it place. But taking twelve time-measurements, that was nonsense, I thought.

V.   Let us discuss your electronic music, *Artikulation* in particular. What is the connection between the technique used in *Artikulation* and the ideas you were developing at the time you left Hungary, e.g. static music?

L.   There is nothing in the way of static sonorities in *Artikulation*. It re-creates the articulated sound of speech, of an unintelligible speech. Since 1950, static music had always been somewhere at the back of my mind. I first tried to express it in *Víziók*, composed in the summer of 1956. But it was only one of several types of musical idiom I entertained. Other ideas were the wildly gesticulating, hectic music, the sound of articulate speech, and machine-like music. While studying at the electronic studios I was also busy learning about phonetics, more exactly about German phonology. I thought I might experiment with the synthetic production of speech sounds. I was greatly influenced – as all musicians in Cologne were – by Meyer-Eppler, professor of phonetics at the University of Bonn, who was also one of the founding members of the Cologne studios. I was planning to produce synthetic vowels and consonants using sine-wave generators, white noise and impulse generators and the filtering equipment we were working with. I built up a collection of minimal sound elements and artificial speech sounds to use as basic raw material for composition. One of the considerations in this work was that, formally speaking, music could be articulated in an analogous way to normal spoken prose. Prior to that I had composed another piece, *Glissandi*, that is much more primitive than *Artikulation*. I planned a third electronic piece, but that was never realized; I called it *Pièce électronique* no. 3 (I was rather keen on French titles in those days). In that piece, I meant to try out a process which I then thought feasible. But it turned out to be impossible. My idea was that a sufficient number of overtones without the fundamental would, as a result of their combined acoustic effect, sound the fundamental. I wanted to select and record on tape overtones between 1,000 Hz and 6,000 Hz, use only these and expected the composite sounds to emerge automatically. I planned to make music out of pure sine-waves with harmonic and subharmonic combinations, by introducing the metallic sound of subharmonics as well as the harmonics gradually, not all at once. I imagined that slowly, different composite sounds would emerge and slowly fade away again like shadows. I intended to produce forty-eight layers of sound. When I tried to do all that in the studio, it turned out to be a quite illusory idea, unfeasible. It dawned on me that the sound I wanted could be realized much more easily with an orchestra. The first title I gave *Pièce électronique* no. 3 was *Atmosphères*. In brief, work in the electronic studios was very interesting and I learned a great deal from it, but realised that it was not for me.

V.   Something has just occurred to me. Around the time that you wrote *Atmosphères* for orchestra, in the early '60s, the idea of working with blocks of basically twelve-note clusters was in the air. There are similar works by other composers dating back to those years. Off hand I can think only of Nono's *Diario polacco*.

L.   There was also Penderecki's *Anaklasis*, Kagel's *Anagrama*, Stockhausen's *Carré*; all of them composed at about the same time. *Atmosphères* was still in rough draft, so *Anaklasis* and *Carré* may have left their mark on it.

V.   I am not so very interested in influences but rather wonder why several composers were working with continuous block sounds in the early '60s. How does all this fit in with Cage's first appearance in Europe? Or were composers simply reacting to serialism? In twelve-note blocks, twelve-note music obviously cancels itself out.

L.   It does. I am certain that the reason why 'static' sound was in the air was, as you have said, that musicians were reacting to serialism and to Cage's aleatory ideas. More exactly, reacting to their basic formal structure, which is: event – pause – event – pause. Continuous sound is at the opposite pole. As for my own music the first movement of *Apparitions* cannot be seen as a reaction to serialism, since my original draft dates back to before my leaving Hungary. Later, having analysed Boulez's *Structures* carefully, it became clear to me that it was impossible further to refine the treatment of rhythm and intervals or to increase the complexity of rhythm, melody and harmony – they had already been pushed to the limit. My answer to this was *Apparitions* and later *Atmosphères*. Should I return to clearer diatonic structures or press on ahead, towards completely blurred outlines of sound? – I wondered. There are rhythmic events in both works but when so many rhythmic processes are superimposed that they cover one another, the result is a homogeneous musical 'mass'. Seen from this angle, with *Atmosphères* I was consciously reacting against the refinement of serialism. Musical texture in *Atmosphères* is also refined but in a quite different dimension.

V.   All commentaries about *Atmosphères* agree on one point, that transformations of timbre are the very essence of the work, a feature that is seen as the continuation of Schoenberg's *Klangfarbenmelodie*. Am I right in thinking that an equally important feature in the work is the movement of lines, the upward or downward moving structure of the parts?

L.   I think that *Atmosphères* represents something new in the way that the timbre is changing continuously. In Webern's Opus 10 a melodic line consists of notes, each of them of different timbre, but that simply amounts to a succession of sounds in which the transformation of timbre is not a continuous process, but proceeds in discrete jumps. As it is not possible to change the timbre of an oboe into that of a violin, I combined the sound of the four oboes with the sound of many violins in such a manner that first you could just discern a faint oboe timbre in the midst of the violins, then the oboe timbre gradually came to dominate the

38

sound. It is not just a matter of changing tone colour but also of the rate of change, the dosage, and the dynamic modification. Modifications of timbre and dynamics are obviously very significant but the patterns emerging from them are even more important. Melody, harmony and rhythm do not constitute the real 'event', which is rather like the slow, gradual transformation of the 'molecular state' of sound or the changing pattern of a kaleidoscope. In my opinion, that is what is new in *Atmosphères*. It is a rather superficial view to lay too much emphasis on timbre. The misunderstanding may have arisen from a sentence in the programme notes I wrote for the first performance in Donaueschingen, 'Die Klangfarben haben formbildende Funktion' – timbre has a structural role in giving form to music. Critics who do not know enough about music often comment on the programme notes instead of on the music they hear. That is how *Atmosphères* came to be considered 'timbre music' and I was put into the same pigeon-hole with Penderecki. In answer to your question I should say that the changes and modifications of the overall pattern are the important feature, not the tone colours. All this really goes back to what I was doing in the electronic studios; I applied what I had learned there to instrumental and vocal music. More exactly, the technique of changing patterns comes from Gottfried Michael Koenig. Koenig synthesized tunes from a number of sine waves. He made use of a well-known acoustic phenomenon. When a series of notes of different pitch are sounded at a rate of over twenty per second, we are able to hear the different pitches but we cannot tell in what order they follow one another. Koenig made up his tunes by splicing small bits of tape together in such a way that the the whole duration was under $\frac{1}{20}$ of a second (fifty milli-seconds); the tune was transformed into a chord; a tune consisting of six notes became a six-note chord. Koenig's other idea was that he kept a given number of notes in a tune under $\frac{1}{20}$ second, below our threshold of perceiving them separately, whilst the whole tune was longer than $\frac{1}{20}$ second. The result was something like seeing the tune through a narrow slit, which was moving forward so that at any time you could hear two or three notes together, which gave the impression of polyphony. It was still a tune but a strangely blurred one. This technique produced a gradually changing pattern. My idea was to apply to instrumental music what I had learned from Koenig in the electronic studio. This was a compositional idea, not an exercise for its own sake, a mere technical device. I wanted to possess, apart from tune, harmony and rhythm, a method of creating transformations in the 'molecular state' of sound. Since you cannot play an instrument fast enough to produce a succession of notes at a rate of twenty per second, I built the rhythmic shifts into the music. For instance, twenty-four violins would play the same tune but with a slight time-lag between them. The figurations were almost identical but not quite. Later I realised that this was nothing new. The string parts at the end of *Walküre* (Feuerzauber) are such that no violonist can play them, all of them make mistakes, different mistakes all the time. These mistakes add up and create a floating, fluctuating pattern, i.e. *Bewegungsfarbe*. Technically, *Atmosphères* is based on the same principle.

V. In *Atmosphères* you worked everything out and noted down all the details exactly. In your next work, *Volumina*, nothing is precisely indicated in the score. What made you employ graphic notation which, after all, isn't an approximate notation?

L. Graphic notation was very fashionable at the time. The Americans were the first to use it, Feldman, Brown, Cage; in Europe, Bussotti also adopted it. I had some reservations. On the whole, I tend to take a good look at innovations and if I do not find any need for them I leave them well alone. In the case of *Atmosphères* the conductor had to have a score fully written out and the members of the orchestra also needed precise notation. Graphic notation or some other new way of writing down music, such as adopted by Penderecki for instance (thick black lines), does not provide enough detail. In *Volumina* an exact indication of pitch is of no importance as the texture consists of clusters, therefore all I needed to do was to define the limits of clusters and indicate how the limits change both in space and in time. The score really has precise indications, apart from the area where some flexibility is required. Any player who observes the instructions in the score will produce much the same sound. By flexibility I mean a kind of rubato both in time and space. Rubato in tempi had been in use for a long time but rubato pitch was then something new. Such elasticity of pitch becomes possible when you write music in which what really matters is not the pitch of the individual notes but the shape of the clusters, their volume and breadth. I tried to find a suitable notation for this in order to be able to note down everything with reasonable precision for the organist. For instance, I can keep one key pressed down with my right thumb and then gradually press down all successive keys

40

with my palm and with my lower arm; this produces an upward growing cluster. Consequently, for right hand clusters you mark the lower limit precisely with a line, whereas the upper limit is indicated approximately with a curve, which shows roughly how to apply the palm and the lower arm to the keyboard. The same applies to the left hand, the notation being the mirror image of that for the right hand. Clusters for the pedals are obviously bound to be narrower. As you can see, such notation does not give much freedom to the interpreter to play as the spirit moves him. Originally graphic notation meant just a piece of paper with some sketches on, which you handed to the soloist telling him to play as he thought best. On one occasion I asked David Tudor, the pianist who specializes in such interpretation, whether he could play *Mona Lisa*. He said, yes he could, but added that Bussotti's sketches were much more amenable to that kind of treatment.

V.   I remember when Tudor performed a Bussotti work at Darmstadt for the first time in 1959, the composer and the soloist had quite a long argument about whose interpretation of the sketches was the right one.

L.   Notation for *Volumina* is not like that. I should call it cluster notation, which is precise but without indication of the individual pitches.

V.   I think that in *Volumina* we find both basic types of your music, the static and the wildly gesticulating.

L.   That is correct.

V.   Am I right in thinking that the way you combine the two types corresponds more or less to a fairly conventional A-B-A-B-A form?

L.   Looking at it in this way, yes it does. If you are just listening for the alternation of the static and the gesticulating type of music, you can easily make out an A-B-A form. But if you look at it from the point of view of pitch you see an entirely different formal structure: the piece has two culminating points in high register. My idea was a form uninterruptedly rolling forward, in which different kinds of musical motion appear either through gradual transformation or with abrupt switches. But I agree that it is possible to reduce it to an A-B-A formula. And that is nothing to be ashamed of. My formulation would not be so very different, since somewhere in the background a passacaglia is reflected in Volumina. Take the exposition, for instance. It is a big mass of sound, which starts very loud, then gradually diminishes and is followed by variations of the original mass.

V.   Could we perhaps indulge in a parenthesis here, as I should like to ask you about overall form in your music.

L.   As I have said earlier I was still in Budapest when I was first struck by a discrepancy between the radical novelty of Bartók's musical material and the traditional forms he used. The shadow of nineteenth-century formal structures is always there in the background of Schoenberg's and Berg's music as well as of Bartók's. Indeed, Webern deliberately composed music in sonata or rondo form, although you cannot really hear it, since it is covered up either by a mesh-like or a crystalline musical texture. Debussy's late works show a way out of this inconsistency, with respect to formal structure not to sound texture. I cannot recall the occasion when I heard *Jeux* for the first time, but in Cologne people kept speaking about it. What is so remarkable about *Jeux* is that it has no 'officially acceptable' form. To go back to an earlier expression of mine, it has not got its tie all neatly tied. It is neither a rondo nor a sonata form, nor an A-B-A ternary form, nor anything else. And yet it has a unity, as its thematic material goes back to the same basic idea. Its form is like vegetation, like a tropical tree whose wildly growing aerial roots grow downwards back into the soil. For me Debussy meant liberation from traditional form, not Schoenberg, Berg or Webern, who in this respect are much more traditional; nor Stravinsky for that matter: in his compositions the suite form is dominant. Even his most progressive music, which is undoubtedly *Le Sacre du Printemps*, consists of very clearly defined short sections – it is really like a suite. Eventually, much later, I discovered Debussy's free formal ideas in Mahler's music; the last movement of his Sixth Symphony, for instance, which is only nominally a sonata-rondo; schematic formal structure does not apply here, it is all broken up, dissolved. Its cohesion comes from the unity of an all-pervasive mood, or perhaps it is due to its thematic material being derived from the same basic pattern, as is the case in the late works of Debussy. It is a new kind of form, a surging flow, yet it is not shapeless. That is what I adopted as my model. While I was in Cologne, I evolved a new approach; I wanted to give my compositions a specific overall form and within it a carefully worked out pattern of smaller units, each with a form of its own. In fact, I had been working along the same lines earlier; if you analyse the first draft of what was to become *Apparitions*, a work called *Víziók*, you find that it progresses through a succession of static block surfaces, alternately played on low or high register instruments. At the time I conceived my music in blocks of this kind, although I did not work them out in numerical proportions but just noted down, rather naïvely, the sound as I imagined it. Although I have never composed serial music, in 1957 I was greatly influenced by the prevailing mood among musicians in Cologne and Darmstadt. I felt the need to work out the construction of my works with great precision. I was in complete agreement with Ernö Lendvai's Bartók analysis. (Just for the record; in the Cologne studios I tried to apply the principle of the golden section to my work with partials. The result was senseless and it sounded awful.) Since then, I have come to the conclusion that the golden section is only one of several formal divisions that are neither quite symmetrical nor quite asymmetrical. In the first movement of *Apparitions*, I applied Bartók's golden section as interpreted by Lendvai. Its first part is in a low register and the second in a high register; the relative duration of the two parts corresponds to the proportions of the golden section. Subsequent shorter parts of the movement are also divided in the same proportion. The golden section is in fact the dominant formal principle of the work. Looking back on it, I must say that I could have applied any other principle of proportions just as well. The general idea of its overall form was a dark block surface followed, through a sudden explosion of light, by a high register block, with the dark block containing elements of the following light one and vice versa. The underlying idea is very visual. The second movement of *Apparitions* is the first example of my use of micropolyphony, which is in fact both a technical and a formal device. Textures moving at different speeds form layers of sound that are very complex. It is the method of gradually changing movement and pattern that is much more explicit in *Atmosphères*. The formal characteristics of *Atmosphères* operate on two levels, internal structure and audible form. The internal structure does not come through, you cannot actually hear it. Both overall form and smaller formal units are divided so as to conform to a certain proportion; I adhered to this proportion down to the smallest formal elements. All this was the manifestation of the constructionist phase I went through in Cologne. It was typical of me that I gave the exact duration of each formal section in seconds and then wrote on the first page of the score that both duration and metronome markings are simply approximate indications. That is what I find the ideal solution, to state the proportions but not to insist on strict observance of them. Since *Atmosphères* I have never worked out proportions with great precision.

V. My idea about a later work, *San Francisco Polyphony*, is that it is a gradual intensification of every musical parameter with a coda at the end.

L. That is one way of looking at it, but I think it is more complex than that. The way I see its structure is this: the exposition of the musical material creates a chromatic space that is filled up with heterogeneous tunes which are different from, and stand in contrast to, one another. The space then gets less dense, as if someone went through it with a comb, thinning it out; the introduction ends on a high note (the introduction to *Melodien* is much the same), then follows the middle section, the longest part of the work, where twisting ostinatos whirl around long, expressive melodies. Gradually the musical texture gets polarized between the higher and lower registers; at the two poles density increases, leaving an expanding empty space in the middle. Ultimately the melodic texture is squashed to the ceiling and the floor and it all ends in a C across several octaves; every tune has been eliminated, as if ironed flat, reduced to one note. At this point the coda begins, a kind of perpetuum mobile machine-like music.

V. Let us get back to the two *Aventures*. Could you tell me about the origin and the form of these two works and their place in your *œuvre*?

L. Originally I intended to write just one piece. I composed it in 1962 and felt that such a concentrated and expressive – expressive and deep-frozen – work cannot be long, so after eleven or twelve minutes I simply cut through the musical form, at an alto solo. In 1965 I started work on *Nouvelles Aventures*. It has two movements; the second is the part I cut off at the end of *Aventures* in 1962. I wrote a first movement, which is in fact a speech composition based on the vowels a, o, œ, e, u, y, i. There are several things at the root of this work. When I was still in Budapest I was very interested in the idea of composing music whose formal characteristics are those of speech. That was part of my wanting to get away from periodic form, from 'rhyming' music. I first realised this idea in the electronic piece, *Artikulation*; that was before my work on 'speech music' in Cologne. I also had literary sources of inspiration in Vienna, but mainly in Cologne; *Sonate mit Urlauten* by Schwitters, Hugo Ball's first Dadaist poems dating back to World War I, the lettrist movement

44

in Paris – Dufrêne, Henri Chopin, Isou. Around 1960 came several compositions influencing me along the same lines; Stockhausen's *Carré*, Kagel's *Anagrama* and some works by Berio and Haubenstock-Ramati. The difference with these – with the exception of *Carré* – is that they all contain intelligible speech. I wrote my own text, which is semantically meaningless and has only emotional content. Music in *Aventures* moves on two distinct levels. One level is constructive; for instance a section may consist only of vowels, or only of liquid consonants; in one section I gradually transform vowels into nasals. There is a section where voiceless consonants are gradually changed into voiced ones and dental consonants into palatals. The other level is the emotional level. I put together a kind of 'scenario' by joining five areas of emotions; humour, ghostly-horror, sentimental, mystical-funereal and erotic. All five areas or processes are present, all through the music, and they switch from one to the other so abruptly and quickly that there is a virtual simultaneity. Each of the three singers plays five roles at the same time. *Aventures* is a very complex piece. It is based on a kind of script which defines the succession – also the simultaneity – of the different emotional situations. On the other hand there is a general construction governing the use of phonetic configurations, i.e. the different patterns of vocal sound. Eventually, the overall form of the piece is almost that of an opera: a succession of short scenes. Moreover, the instrumental parts complement the phonetic patterns: there are meticulously composed instrumental and vocal contrapuntal structures; one at the beginning, for instance, which has the title 'Conversation' (it is a vocal trio without instrumental parts) is virtually a strict Bach three-part invention, whose subjects appear in each voice in different permutations. In 1957 I went for a walk with Stockhausen and spoke about this plan. He thought it would be better to realize it in the medium of electronic music. His suggestion led to *Artikulation*, which is the first version of *Aventures*.

V. Did your 'wildly gesticulating' music also come from that?

L. It has its roots in *Artikulation* and *Volumina* or perhaps most clearly in *Aventures*, which I wrote immediately after *Volumina*.

V. Is it also the first appearance of another of your later musical types, the meccanico?

L. Yes, I think I have mentioned earlier that a short section of *Nouvelles Aventures*, Les Horloges Démoniaques, is the first example of meccanico music. It is the section composed in 1962.

By the way, the speech-like 'articulate' music in *Aventures* led to a later work, the second movement of the Cello Concerto, which is some kind of *Aventures* without words, the cello being the speaker.

V. My next question is meant to lead us to the Requiem. Practically all analysts of your music say that there is a great deal of similarity, almost an identity between *Aventures*, especially the Allegro appassionato movement, and the *Dies irae* of the Requiem, although they reflect two completely different spheres of emotion and mood.

L. I do not think that you can speak about different emotional spheres. You find the same hectic, frenetic 'stile concitato' in the *Dies irae* and *Aventures*, only the former has words while the latter has no intelligible text. Both express the same emotional content.

V. Projecting the Requiem's style back onto *Aventures*, would you say that the Allegro appassionato of *Aventures* also strikes the terrifying note of the Last Judgement?

L. The idea of the Last Judgement was a constant preoccupation with me for many years, without any reference to religion. Its main features are the fear of death, the imagery of dreadful events and a way of cooling them, freezing them through alienation, which is the result of excessive expressiveness. Do not forget that the two *Aventures* and the Requiem date back to the same period. These three works constitute one group; and *Le Grand Macabre* also belongs together with them.

V. The list of your compositions and also some of your remarks indicate that you started setting the text of the Requiem to music while you were still living in Budapest. Why did you so often return to this text since, as you say, your opera is also an instance of your interest in it?

L. Let us concentrate on the *Dies irae*. I have always been fascinated by the idea of hell and scenes of the Last Judgement. I am thinking of Brueghel and especially of Bosch, whose paintings present a mixture of fear and grotesque humour; you find the same mood in his pictures that do not represent the Last Judgement, such as the *Garden of Earthly Delights* in the Prado. In Kafka's writings too, horror is often laced with humour. Gregor Samsa's transformation into a gigantic insect is both dreadful and humorous. As a line of free association, I could mention a film cartoon I remember in which Mickey Mouse, who is up against the cat, pumps the air into his biceps to make himself strong enough to punch the cat in the face really hard, as if he said, 'I'll teach these demons who terrify me'. I am also thinking of Steinberg's cartoons, ominous landscapes with crocodiles lurking everywhere ready to swallow you at any moment; at the same time it is all rather funny, since the cartoons look like children's drawings in crayon. Another writer comes to mind, Boris Vian (although I did not know him at the time I was working on the Requiem), *The Froth of Days*, *Autumn in Peking*. Vian is a humorous brother of Kafka. Going back to paintings, Magritte's surrealist pictures are really like reality carried to the utmost limit, an exact representation of certain forms of madness, distorted perspectives, everything machine-like. As a child I was very frequently afraid, but in my imagination I created a world in which I found relief from terror. During my first years at school I hardly noticed the real world, I transformed clouds into huge mountains, giving them all names. Going to school I always imagined that I was flying in an aeroplane over my imaginary kingdom; stones along the kerb were the skyscrapers seen from above. I lived in an imaginary world. That is probably why Thomas of Celano's *Sequence for the Dead* caught my fancy later in my teens. I always thought I should write a Requiem Mass just for the *Dies irae*. In a drawing I once made, long before composing the Requiem, you can see the Archangel Michael on the Day of Judgement weighing the souls on a balance from the butcher's shop; the Devil in the shape of a spider catches the souls, netting them like butterflies. In the late '40s I made two plans for a Requiem. The first idea that I worked out, while I was a student at the Academy, was to have a chorus accompanied by harps and percussion, practically a Requiem with cuckoo accompaniment, but I meant it as a serious work not as a joke. The idea probably came from something I had heard during the war, or perhaps just after the war. János Hammerschlag got together a number of musicians and a large choir for a performance of a work by Pérotin. As there are no indications in the score as to what instruments to use, Hammerschlag duplicated the human voice with all kinds of percussion, a Glockenspiel as well as all kinds of bells. Pérotin was transformed into a mixture of church music and fair-ground music. My first draft for a Requiem is in an archaic kind of Bartók style. In the early '50s I started work on another draft; it is twelve-note music although I did not know Schoenberg or Webern but had heard about their music and worked out a kind of pentatonic serialism. The series consisted of two pentatonic scales – with two pien[6] notes they add up to twelve. At about the same time I was making plans for an oratorio to the text of Sándor Weöres's *Istar's Journey to Hell*. It began with a machine-like passacaglia; the bass was a twelve-note series and various versions of the twelve-note series, moving at various speeds, tore into the bass line like a cogwheel.

V. May I interrupt you here? How far did different settings of the Requiem that you knew influence your early drafts?

L. I think not at all. I knew Mozart's and Verdi's Requiems but not Berlioz's or Cherubini's. But I was not influenced by Mozart or Verdi but by Pérotin and Machaut. At the time I turned to archaic styles, I composed a lot of organum music, not based on fourths or fifths, of course, but using, say, a tritone progression. I was aiming at very 'tight' parallels and also used the cogwheel device I mentioned just now. I feel sure that my later meccanico style has its origin in these compositions.

V. How does all that tie up with the commission to write the Requiem which prompted you actually to do it?

L. Here I have to go back to the sounding of my 'internal bells!' In Stockholm, in 1961, I was told about the possible commission to write a substantial work for choir and orchestra for the tenth anniversary of the New Music Series. That sounded the bell in me and I suggested that I might do a Requiem, although a Requiem is not particularly suited to a jubilee concert, particularly as it was not meant to be the last concert of the series. The idea was accepted. At the time I was thinking in terms of a full Requiem Mass. There were compositional reasons for its actual final shape: just four movements, including a separate *Lacrimosa* as the epilogue. Immediately after the Requiem I composed *Lux aeterna* in a slightly different style, but it is part of the same general requiem idea.

V. My next question may surprise you but I am going to ask it all the same. We are used in traditional vocal works to music that depicts the mood of the text by musical means. I have the impression that also in several passages of your Requiem you

---

[6] Pien: in Chinese music it denotes the two notes that are a semitone below the fifth degree and the octave note respectively of a diatonic scale. (e.g. f sharp and b on a scale c to c'.) Often used by modern writers with reference to other kinds of music (e.g. Gregorian Chant) in which certain degrees of the scale are considered less important than others and therefore are treated as mere ornamental or passing tones [notes].

Harvard Dictionary, rev. 2nd edn., W. Apel, 1970

intend to depict the words in music.

L.   Almost as in madrigals.

V.   Perhaps the most salient example of such a treatment is in what I find a rather surprising passage in *Tuba Mirum*, when the mezzo-soprano solo, on reaching the word 'sepulchra', goes down to the lowest note. But when the same idea is expressed in other words you give it a quite different melodic treatment. Another example is the open melodic line of *Salva me* and particularly the whole of the *Lacrimosa*.

L.   Certainly. In the *Dies irae* I saw the Sequence as a colourful picture-book, with new images conjured up all the time, in every third line. Here I definitely wanted to paint pictures in music; my aim was a virtually visual representation.

V.   That is what I also find in the *Introitus*, as the music rises from the darkness of *Requiem aeternam* to the light of *Lux perpetua*.

L.   That was also intentional. That is why I gave such prominence to the double bass clarinet in the orchestration; combined with the double-basses it gives a strange, metallic vibration. There is another line in the text, 'et lux perpetua luceat eis', which also evoked in me essential images in colour; eight-note chords played on six double-basses and two cellos, all of them sounding fairly low harmonics. This combination produces a glassy translucence, which also gives the effect of 'dark' light. In the end it really sounded as I had imagined it, although at the time the combined sound of low double-bass harmonics in a chord was a quite new effect. The entire work is pervaded by such allusive elements, associations, reminiscent of madrigals.

V.   It is just as natural then that the *Kyrie*-fugue is of a completely consistent, homogeneous musical texture.

L.   Yes, indeed. The text is neutral, free from imagery. In this movement I wanted to combine Flemish polyphony with my own new micropolyphony. I took Ockeghem as my model, and adopted his 'varietas' principle, where the voices are similar without being identical. It is true that the fugue did not exist in Ockeghem's time and, structurally speaking, this movement is a strange twenty-part fugue. The twenty parts are divided into five groups, each of them a four-part canon. The canonic parts are identical in their notes but their rhythmic articulations are always different and no rhythmic pattern is ever repeated in a canon. I think that here I succeeded in realizing Ockeghem's 'varietas' principle. I had worked out for myself beforehand a set of rules both for the melodic lines and for the harmonic structure, rules that are almost as strict as those of the Flemish composers or Palestrina's. For instance, the permutation of the rhythmic patterns, which is reminiscent of methods employed in serialism although the *Kyrie*-fugue is not serial music. Working on the composition was rather like weaving a carpet, some parts ready, some threads still hanging loose: and then I would go on weaving according to the rules I prescribed for myself. At any given point there were several possibilities of how to go on; I chose one and went on weaving the smaller patterns of the canons and the larger ones of the fugue.

V.   Summing it all up, the descriptive musical portrayal reminiscent of madrigals, the strict rules like those of Flemish composers applied to the construction of the *Kyrie*, the hocket technique in parts of the *Dies irae*, I can confidently say of you that you are at once a contemporary composer and a traditionalist, a composer who respects tradition and yet is of our times. To use a fashionable term, you transcend tradition by preserving it.

L.   Many composers find this Hegelian concept of 'Aufhebung', the dichotomy of affirmation-rejection, inconsistent. They feel that a choice must be made between tradition and progress. But I experiment with new forms, new timbres...

V.   I do not like the expression experimental work, or even the word experiment. In my view a creative artist would not present a work that he regards as an experiment.

L.   I keep experimenting and, however conceited it may sound, my experiments are always successful.

V.   Going back to what we said earlier about transcending and preserving, or, as you put it, affirmation-rejection, was the return to tradition on several levels something that the very genre of the Requiem inspired you to do, or is it characteristic of your works in general?

L.   It did not come from the genre; pieces that are in no way traditional, such as the two *Aventures*, also contain many traditional elements. One passage in *Nouvelles Aventures*, for instance, is really a two-part twelve-note chorale worked out according to Hindemith's principles in *Unterweisung im Tonsatz*, but it is deliberately and completely muddled up. There are also many traditional elements in the Second Quartet and in the *Ten Pieces for Wind Quintet*. The entire string quartet tradition from Beethoven to Webern is there somewhere in the quartet, even sonata-form, although only like an immured corpse. *Volumina* is a structure left empty, the music is somehow left empty; there is room for melodies in it, everything is ready to receive the thematic elements and motifs and yet they remain conspicuously absent. It is not irony but rather like looking through the wrong end of a telescope. In this respect I am both for tradition and against it. I could almost go so far as to say that I lack the quality of frantic search for something new to say all the time that is characteristic of many of my fellow musicians.

V. Here we could perhaps make a short disgression and introduce another point. You are obviously not the only one to notice the dichotomy of tradition and modernism in your work. It must have struck the critics as well. But I do not suppose you care much . . .

L. Oh, but I do.

V. It is strange to find a composer who is not indifferent to what the critics say – to strike a note of self-irony.

L. A composer who says that he is not interested in critical opinion is lying.

V. What niche have they found to put you in?

L. They find it difficult to fit me into a pigeon-hole. They do not know what to do with me. I mean the average critic, since there are outstanding critics who do not work in terms of pigeon-holes. But, on the whole, critical opinion assumes that there are always groups, like the Fives, the Sixes, the neoclassical school, the Viennese school, the serialist school, the aleatory school; they feel they have to stick a label on everybody. As I am not labelled, they often do not quite understand what I am after. Also, many people are disturbed by the mixture of serious and funny elements, they do not understand it, they have no sense of humour. Composers also need to make use of some jargon, if they want to be 'in'. In the egg, I should say. Anyway, every five or six years you get new people in the egg; the main thing is that you must always be very modern. People are also afraid to criticise something they do not understand, because you never know what will come of it.

V. That is exactly what I meant to ask you. How do the critics regard your work, or rather the indefinable combination of what is traditional in it and what is not?

L. Not very favourably on the whole. They do not like it at all if somebody is a modern composer and yet does not relinquish the past. How should I put it? There are official composers who dress up in a dinner suit and Bohemian ones who wear jeans. I do not wear either. In every country and every system there are official composers and the complete outsiders. It seems very disturbing that I do not belong to either group. In spite of that I usually get very good reviews but most critics are discomfited by my not fitting into either mould. What can I do? My position in this respect is the same as what I have said about my music, I think. There must be some kind of order, but not too much of it and it should not be dogmatic. But there must not be disorder either. The beginning of the *San Francisco Polyphony*, for instance, is very chaotic, but it is a somehow stratified chaos. Or think of the chords in *Le Grand Macabre*. I use certain types of chords but they are all slightly flawed, there is always something out of place. It gives the same impression as when you enter a room and see that all the pieces of furniture had been placed carefully but the cleaning woman is not quite the best and has pushed them all out of place a little.

V. You completed *Lux aeterna* in 1966 and your next vocal work dates from 1973. During the seven intervening years you composed only instrumental music. Was there a special reason for this or did it just happen like that?

L. It was not intentional. In fact, I was planning to work on the opera after *Aventures* in 1965.

V. Let us go on to the Cello Concerto. What struck me as a very important feature in it was the re-discovery of the octave, which has already come up in our conversation. You have said that the musical material in the second movement of this concerto is much the same as in *Aventures* only without words. Is there anything else you could add about the Cello Concerto?

L. The Concerto has two movements, the second being a variant of the first. The musical material presented in the first movement is followed by a great crescendo. At the end of the crescendo the orchestra suddenly stops as if torn off and the cello goes on by itself. The notes climb higher and higher, to the fourteenth harmonic and beyond. I wanted to emphasize the height and enhance the impression of empty spaces yawning below by having the double-bass play on – the only instrument that is left from the orchestra – so that an almost infinite space opens up between the two registers. My intention was to create the impression of a vast soap-bubble that may burst at any moment. A corresponding part comes at the end of the second movement – a variant of the first – where the successive 'conferences' of the instruments are followed by a great crescendo, then again the cello is left alone to play a whispering cadence, sul ponticello harmonics, extremely rapid passages getting fainter and fainter until they finally vanish. I may mention that in almost all my works you find what you could call a 'danger zone', such as the high cello harmonics I have just referred to. I like pushing things to the limit of the possible. Performers have often said, 'you cannot play this piece' or 'it is impossible to sing it'. My answer always was, 'it is almost impossible, but just try and you'll almost make it'. On one occasion when rehearsals for my Requiem were going on in Stockholm, I received a telegram asking me to go there because the choir was unable to sing the fugue in the *Kyrie*. In fact they were perfectly capable of singing it, only they were taking everything too strictly, they wanted to render the septuplets precisely. I explained to the choir that it was all right if they did not sing all the notes exactly; all they had to do was to approximate to what they saw in the score both rhythmically and melodically and that it did not matter if they made little mistakes – the mistakes had been reckoned with. Whereas I wrote down everything precisely I was aware that the choir could not sing it all exactly. My reason for so 'overwriting' the score was to achieve the effect I wanted, a sense of danger. I used the twelve-note chromatic scale in the *Kyrie*. But what you actually hear is not a chromatic scale, since the singers cannot help making mistakes in the intonation, which produces a kind of microtonality, dirty patches; and these 'dirty patches' are very important (if they follow the score too loosely that is also wrong, the result will be too dirty). Listening to this piece, what you hear is not the twelve-note chromatic scale but all kinds of other intervals. Hence the difference between the score and what you hear. Many people have objected to my noting down everything in the score with such precision. My answer is that, first of all, I am an obsessional neurotic and people should tolerate my little peculiarities; secondly, if I do not put down everything with such precision the result will not be as I intended, there will be a discrepancy.

V. You will excuse my interrupting you but one cannot help asking the question: why did you not want the music performed as you noted it down in the score; what made you work all those mistakes into it, all the wrong intonations of the singers?

L. My intention was to abandon the tempered scale. In the Requiem I used the method of working little mistakes into the score. In a later piece, *Ramifications*, I divided the strings into two groups with a quarter-tone difference in the intonation between them. This did not produce music based on quarter-tones; that was not my intention. In any case the difference between 440 and 453 is slightly more than a quarter-tone. The point is that as the two groups of strings, deliberately tuned apart from one another, go on playing the group tuned higher automatically slides downwards so that the two groups get nearer one another in pitch. That is what I wanted: not music based on quarter-tones but mistuned music.

V. Another question. Whereas you wanted and perhaps still want to get away from temperament, you have not returned to electronic music, although it would offer this possibility.

L. I want to abandon equal temperament because I think it is a worn-out medium. Listening to a harpsichord or an organ tuned in the mean-tone system you can make out perfect intervals that would never occur in equal temperament – they make a miraculous sound effect. For a time I was very interested in the music of Harry Partch, an American composer who is hardly known in Europe. I even went to see him in 1972. He made new instruments or changed the tuning of others so as to get pure harmonics. His actual compositions are not particularly interesting, but harmonically speaking they are very exciting. All those real major chords, dominant and ninth chords, major thirds, which are tighter than in equal temperament and the minor sevenths, well, they sound quite ethereal. The way Partch uses his instruments, all tuned differently, is that each produces perfectly pure sound with natural harmonics but, from the point of view of equal temperament, they are outrageously out of tune in relation to one another. That is what interested me, the effect of music where the tuning systems clash; it is like a body in a state of gradual decomposition. You can hear such 'Partch effects' in my Double Concerto for flute and oboe. You ask me why I like that kind of music. Liszt said on one occasion that he was only interested in music that had at least one quite new modulation, that no one had used before. My feeling is that both diatonic and chromatic music have been worn out. I do not think we need to look for other tonal systems – I abhor all fixed systems; what I really want is the effect of deviation from either pure or equal temperament. I have tried to achieve this effect in different ways in my works. We have already spoken about *Ramifications*. In the Second Quartet some notes have to be intoned either higher or lower. In the Double Concerto you can push the notes of the flute higher or lower by a special manipulation of the stops. Of course, you cannot formulate hard and fast rules for this method; in any case it is not always feasible. In my opera, practical considerations made me stick to equal temperament. The same applies to the piano concerto I am now working on. In the Chamber Concerto you automatically get a micro-intervallic deviation, since you can never find a piano, a celesta and an organ all tuned exactly to the same temperament. I must repeat again: I am not dogmatic about it. The fact is that we must not expect all music to conform to equal temperament.

V. All that we have said refers back to what you mean about wanting order with a small admixture of disorder, does it not?

L. Exactly. You asked me why I worked mistakes into the Requiem. I may have given a satisfactory answer, but I should add that statistically speaking there will be hardly any difference between various performances; the smudginess both in intonation and in rhythm gives the same result, the same degree of 'dirtiness'. If you have a sufficiently great number of parts then the various 'approximations' will cancel one another out.

V. Then I think we both agree about those 'Darmstadtians' who write down quite impossible rhythmic configurations.

L. Which you cannot play anyway. I remember one of the first things that struck me in Cologne was when I saw a score (do not let us worry about who the composer was) with a metronomic indication of 52.8. There is a task for a conductor.

V. I do not want to mention the composer by name who starts one of his works with the last semiquaver of a quintuplet.

L. You probably know Gerard Hoffnung's wonderful satirical piece on Darmstadt about two German professors discussing how you can play a low B on the viola, which is simply beyond the instrument's range; and speaking about a bar in 3/4 – the way that a three crotchet rest lends it a Viennese waltz character!

V. Shall we go on to *Lontano* for a full orchestra, which is next in our list of compositions? You have explained in your articles and comments that the title means far away, 'in the distance', which refers to a spatial distance in that each layer of music has yet another layer behind it in the background. You may find my question strange, but does the title not mark some event in time, or rather, age?

L. Both in space and in time. You have late romantic sonorities, Mahler, Bruckner, Wagner. Hans Christian von

Dadelsen, a student of mine, analysed it and found quite a number of fairly close references in it to the Prelude to *Parsifal*. These were not intentional on my part.

V. When I first heard a broadcast of *Lontano* it evoked in me associations with *Rheingold*. You yourself have mentioned Bruckner, Mahler, Wagner. There is a point in *Lontano* where the music reaches a bare octave on D and then the basses come in with a melody. This reminds me of Bartók and brings me back to the question whether the title refers to distance in time?

L. No, that was not the idea. I rather imagined a vast space of sound in gradual transformation, not through dense chromaticism but through a constantly changing pattern of colour like a moiré fabric. Although *Lontano* encompasses the entire chromatic scale, strictly speaking, it is based on a diatonic scale. As I have said, the changes happen in space, the sound of drawing nearer and moving away again. But you are right that there is a second plane on which the music moves in time – quite deliberately. I do not actually quote composers, only allude to nineteenth-century music, evoking late Romantic orchestral effects. The orchestration is such as to make it sound like an organ; the changes are similar to changes of register on an organ. The idea was also to make it reminiscent of Bruckner's orchestral effects.

V. Another point about *Lontano*. Writing about it you have mentioned that underneath the main texture of the music there are slowly emerging melodic fragments; first they are barely discernible but eventually they come to dominate the texture. Which reminds me of what Dallapiccola said, that nobody had taught him more about composition than Joyce and Proust. He gave an example from Proust's *Remembrance of Things Past*, where a character first appears in a passing reference, then fifty pages on we hear more about him and only later when his name comes up for the third or fourth time does he actually enter the stage, is he woven into the narrative proper. Dallapiccola adopted this technique and that is what you are talking about.

L. I have never heard of that, although I like Proust immensely. But now you mention it, I realise that Dallapiccola is quite right.

V. At this point may we digress again? It gives me the opportunity to ask whether your music shows the influence not of other composers but of literature and of the fine arts?

L. I mentioned Krudy when we spoke about the meccanico-type music. Krudy influenced me also in another way (I feel that Krudy and Proust have quite a lot in common). Your example

56

from Proust applies to Krudy, although not in the same way. Márai writes in his *Sindbad* that Krudy wrote his novels sitting in an out of the way little bistro somewhere in Obuda. When he finished a chapter, he handed the manuscript to the waiter to take to the office of the paper that serialized it, then he went on writing the novel but not having the manuscript could not consult earlier chapters. Sometimes a character is mentioned once and then never reappears again in the same novel but we meet him in another novel, which is Proust's method taken one stage further. That is the kind of disorder that has appeared again and again in our conversation, the tie with the untidy knot. Krudy is undoubtedly the main literary influence in my work. I like Proust but I was also influenced by Joyce, especially by *Finnegans Wake*. I could not make it out by myself, my English is not good enough for that. In my Cologne days a small circle of friends met once a week, Koenig, Kagel, Helms, Evangelisti, Metzger the critic and myself, and we read *Finnegans Wake* carefully, just like people studying texts in a Talmud school, finding various interpretations. What impressed me in Joyce at the period when I was working on *Aventures* was his way of treating language as raw material; otherwise his mentality in general is not my cup of tea. If you want to know about literary influences on my compositions and more about my favourite writers then I should mention above all Kleist, the precision of his style, the way he describes dreadful, unbelievable things in a cool, precise manner. This idea arose when we spoke about Kafka. The deep-frozen expressionism was partly triggered off in me by Kleist's and Kafka's style of writing, which is really the exact opposite of Krudy's influence. Here I come back to the idea I have mentioned several times, how the two opposites of precision and sloppiness are both fundamentally part of me. I should also mention Alfred Jarry; his kind of surrealism is the background to *Le Grand Macabre*.

V. Where do you find surrealistic elements in your works? Only in your deep-frozen expressionism, or is it present in other ways too?

L. Yes, in its colourful quality and also in so far as my music is quite free from abstractions. In general, my works abound in images, visual associations, associations of colours, optical effects and forms.

V. Would it be correct to assume that in a piece of yours that is simply called Second Quartet we could also find visual or other associations? Something that would be a private reference and

57

the audience could not understand it?

L. Oh, no, the audience would also have access to it. Just think of the meccanico movement of the Second Quartet.

V. That is too obvious a case.

L. The same applies to the other movements. In the last movement, for instance, an agitato starts up, but you have the impression of seeing and hearing it through a curtain or as if it were all enveloped in a mist. The experiences of listening and seeing come very close and such associations are generally felt rather than being of a purely private kind.

V. I did not want to suggest that it is programme music, not at all... But is there anything that is not programme music?

L. *The Art of Fugue* or the Mozart and Haydn quartets are not really programme music, they are pure musical forms. But associations are not out of the question.

V. I am not thinking about the audience but about you.

L. Well, of course, I do have associations. I am inclined to synaesthetic perception. I associate sounds with colours and shapes. Like Rimbaud, I feel that all letters have a colour.

V. Have you ever tried to work out whether there is any system in your synaesthetic experiences?

L. Oh, yes. Major chords are red or pink, minor chords are somewhere between green and brown. I do not have perfect pitch, so when I say that C minor has a rusty red-brown colour and D minor is brown this does not come from the pitch but from the letters C and D. I think it must go back to my childhood. I find, for instance, that numbers also have colours; 1 is steely grey, 2 is orange, 5 is green. At some point these associations must have got fixed, perhaps I saw the green number 5 on a stamp or on a shop sign. But there must be some collective associations too. For most people the sound of a trumpet is probably yellow although I find it red because of its shrillness. I think, generally speaking, people perceive low register sounds as dark, black and higher ones as lighter or white.

V. At this point let us turn for a moment to the visual arts.

L. Bosch and Brueghel have come up in our conversation several times. I also mentioned cartoon films; my *Ten Pieces for Wind Quintet* constitute really a series of colourful cartoons (from the point of view of associations). I also spoke about the influence surrealist painting and Magritte in particular exercised on my works, especially on *Le Grand Macabre*.

V. How does the transition from a visual impression to the

58

auditory take place?

L. A closer examination of the opera reveals a number of references to the real world; they are like signals. Before Nekrotzar comes on in scene 2, his arrival is announced by the stylised sound of a fire-engine horn. I took care to include the Doppler effect in the music: as the fire engine passes by the stage the pitch goes down by a semitone. In another scene with Nekrotzar I composed a kind of synthetic folk music whose actual constituent elements are genuine folk tunes. Nekrotzar is accompanied by four musicians, four masked devils. One is a violinist who plays a Scott Joplin-type ragtime on his violin which is deliberately mistuned. The bassoon player intones a distorted Greek Orthodox hymn. That is the tune we used to sing at Easter at the Romanian secondary school where I was a pupil (I do not know if the hymn is of Byzantine origin or later). The third devil plays a mixture of a Brazilian and Spanish half samba, half flamenco tune on his E-flat clarinet, the fourth plays on his piccolo a march that is half Scottish, half Hungarian, more exactly a Hungarian pentatonic tune that is made to sound like bagpipe music, and the overall harmonic structure is twelve-note. The orchestral accompaniment consists of a three-layered cha-cha, each layer in different tempo. None of the tunes appeared in its original form, they are not quotations but rather fantasies, reminiscences as worked through the imagination. There are actually exact quotations in the opera; in scene 2, for instance, the cancan from Offenbach's *Orpheus* is played simultaneously with Schumann's *Merry peasant*, although I have changed both, adding a verbunkos or Hungarian recruiting song at the end.

V. Is that what you mean by surrealism in music?

L. Yes it is. I take bits of actual music or signals, put them in an unfamiliar context, distort them, not necessarily making them sound humorous but interpreting them through distortion just as a surrealist painting presents the world. Speaking about the visual arts, I want to go back to cartoonists, to Steinberg or Roland Topor the French caricaturist of demoniac powers of imagination. And they themselves take us back to Bosch and Brueghel, to images that are both horrifying and colourful, that we spoke about in connection with the *Dies irae*.

V. Everything seems to tie up with everything else.

After this disgression let us go back to the chronological survey of your works. The next work is *Continuum*, for harpsichord. We have already spoken about it but there is another point that interests me. *Continuum* starts with a third. Would this music be the first instance of the fully developed preciso, meccanico-type structure and at the same time herald the initial bars of *Clocks and Clouds*?

L.   As we have discussed the meccanico several times I would rather say something more about the initial bars. Several of my works dating back to that period start with a very simple pattern. You'll remember that the Cello Concerto starts on one note, which gradually becomes a minor second; I say gradually, because first there is a floating pitch, a slow deviation. This is also a very simple model which gradually grows more elaborate. In my music this takes the place, and quite intentionally, so to speak, of thematic development. (I find it quite easy to make up beautiful tunes and then elaborate on them but I think that this compositional device is very stale.) The simple models at the start of a composition may be intervals, a minor third, as in *Continuum*, a unison as in the Cello Concerto or in *Lontano* and *Lux aeterna* or a perfect fifth as in the first Organ Study. The point is not using one specific interval; there are several ways of starting a work instead of introducing a subject. If you think of a much later work, the first of my *Three Pieces for Two Pianos*, it starts on an A spread out over four octaves, then an F sharp is added to it, resulting in a minor third which goes on for a while and then gradually other notes enter and the intervallic relationship becomes more complex. The first bars of *Continuum* are much the same. The initial minor third is slowly blurred by the appearance of other intervals, then this complexity clears away and gradually a major second comes to dominate. Perhaps I should add that my compositions dating back to the late '60s have a similar structure; perfect intervals are divided by blurred areas, so that you hear an interval that gets gradually blurred and in the ensuing mist another interval appears, it becomes clearer and clearer until the surrounding mist completely clears and you hear the new interval all by itself.

V.   So a perfect interval marks both the beginning and the end of each formal unit.

L.   Exactly. My idea was that instead of tension-resolution, dissonance-consonance, dominant-tonic, pairs of opposition in traditional tonal music, I would contrast 'mistiness' with passages of 'clearing-up'. 'Mistiness' usually means a contrapuntal texture, a micropolyphonic cobweb technique; the perfect interval appears in the texture first as a hint and then gradually becomes the dominant feature. I should like to add something to my remarks

60

about *Continuum*. Here what you perceive as rhythm is not rhythm coming from the succession of notes your fingers play. The actual rhythm of the piece is a pulsation that emerges from the distribution of the notes, from the frequency of their repetitions. I can perhaps better explain this by taking a concrete example. Both left and right hands play F sharp and G sharp alternately, a kind of trill, then a D sharp appears, the left hand now playing G sharp, F sharp, D sharp, F sharp, while the right hand still alternates F sharp with G sharp. The D sharp stands out, resulting in a ticking, then the right hand also starts playing D sharps in the sequence, the ticking speeds up; the accelerando of the rhythm is therefore the result of an increased frequency of a note, it is realized through a modified note distribution. I used the same technique in the second movement of the Double Concerto and in the first movement of the Chamber Concerto.

V.   The next work chronologically is the Second Quartet, which we have discussed in some detail, so let us go on to *Ten Pieces for Wind Quintet*. I have the feeling that here we have another, different manifestation of how traditional music survives in your work and leads a subterranean existence. Five out of ten pieces are really mini-concertos for each of the wind instruments. My impression is that in these micro concertos you preserve the character of the wind instruments as we know it from Classical and Romantic music. I am referring to such commonplaces as that the horn is a singing instrument, the bassoon is humorous, etc. Was that your intention?

L.   Yes it was. I saw the instruments as five characters or 'personalities' and I gave each of them one movement in which to play a dominant role; each instrument plays what is its most characteristic sound. Not only in the sense of sound quality but also from the point of view of technique. I did not use the Bartolozzi technique[7] although I was familiar with it. In the clarinet part I made use of the specific virtuoso possibilities of this instrument, jumping with the utmost speed from lowest register to overblowing at the third harmonic and back again. In the technique of composing music for the clarinet I learned very much from Richard Strauss and Stravinsky. In one movement, which is a horn solo, I make full use of the cantabile character of the horn, using also the sound contrasts between open, half-stopped and fully stopped notes.

[7] Bruno Bartolozzi systematized a new technique for producing chords on certain instruments (tr.)

V.   *Ramifications* is your next work but it has already appeared in the course of our conversation. As to its overall formal structure I see it as a Classical A-B-A ternary form with a coda. In any case that is what the movement of the music suggests.

L.   That is not how I see it. I have a feeling that you often interpret the form of a work in a particular way although several other interpretations could be applied to it just as easily. I have, in the past, used Classical forms quite deliberately, as in the first movement of *Nouvelles Aventures*. It may be the same with *Ramifications* but it was not my intention. I see it rather as a process of gradual transformation in the form of A-B-C-D-F, in which some sections are variants of A. It could hardly be a ternary form without a repeat, and repeats are something I detest: it is a device that is quite worn out, like sonata form.

V.   Next comes the Chamber Concerto, the first of your longer compositions to be performed in Hungary. I have a theoretical question about the first movement. You have repeatedly stated, both in our conversation and in your writings, that you are against aleatory techniques. And yet in this movement there are cadenza-like passages in small notes and in these you give a certain degree of freedom to the performer. In a later work, the *San Francisco Polyphony*, as I was listening to it (I did not have the score) I also had the impression that some passages are to a certain extent aleatory. Would this mean something like what you said about the fugue of the *Kyrie* in your Requiem, considering that the score of the Chamber Concerto gives quite a lot of latitude to the performer in letting him choose how to play?

L.   It is not really a freedom of choice. At the time I was interested in the idea of multilayered structures, polyrhythm, and beyond that different tempi, different speeds all simultaneously executed. The problem was how to realize it in practice. It was not a new idea at all – I think it already occurs in the first movement of Mahler's First Symphony, in the introduction, and of course in Ives who is the best example of how to employ such a technique. But the first example is in Mozart's *Don Giovanni*, the great imbroglio. The three orchestras are synchronized by means of common higher-level bars but the resulting metrical structure is very intricate. The fundamental idea is that several layers, several processes and movements take place on several planes at the same time. Everything must be held together or else it gets completely out of control. The way I solved the problem in *Melodien*, a later work than the Chamber Concerto, was that,

62

within the overall framework of the 4/4 time signature and the tempo the conductor would control, I indicated different tempi for various instruments by triplets, quintuplets, septuplets, etc. In the first movement of the Chamber Concerto the passages written in small notes simply indicate that the player should execute them as fast as he can. That is why I said that the instrumentalists were not given much freedom; what I kept under strict control was the overall sound texture at any one time. The pitch repertory of each instrument is identical. When for instance one instrument plays C, E flat, F, A flat, and another plays some other permutation of the same notes very rapidly, then the two parts merge into one and the same chord.

V.   I take it then you reject even the 'charge' of a guided chance technique?

L.   No, I do not. Guided aleatory composition – I think that is a good way of putting it. Aleatory in any case is a very loose term. At one extreme you have Cage. Then there is the kind employed by Lutoslawski, where again the pitch-register is strictly controlled, whereas the rhythm follows a more or less random pattern, although taken as a whole it is predictable.

V.   I meant Lutoslawski's method of what we called guided aleatory composition.

L.   In the Chamber Concerto, I used a slightly different method. I didn't prescribe a certain number of repetitions for a particular sequence, to obtain, through this montage, a pattern. I broke down vertical chords and reconstituted them through horizontal parts. Lutoslawski's contrapuntal aleatory music interests me but I have never used it the way he does. The Chamber Concerto certainly ties up in some way with Lutoslawski's kind of aleatory pieces, but there is much less left to chance. When you indicate that the clarinet part should be played as fast as possible you know what the upper limit of speed will be. It is of little importance if a player takes one tenth of a second less to get through a figuration.

Consequently, the difference between exact notation and such freedom of interpretation is minimal. Practically all performances of the movement in question in the Chamber Concerto were essentially identical. Freedom here is a bit like driving a coach and six and slackening the rein; all six horses still run at much the same speed, as each of them conforms to the speed of the others.

V.   At the memorable first performance of the Chamber Concerto in Budapest I was not the only one struck by the end of the

63

first movement, when not only perfect octaves are sounded but there are also hints of incipient melodies.

L. My general idea for that movement was the surface of a stretch of water, where everything takes place below the surface. The musical events you hear are blurred; suddenly a tune emerges and then sinks back again. For a moment the outlines seem quite clear, then everything gets blurred once more. I developed this method in *Melodien*, where the tunes appear much more clearly outlined. In *Melodien*, the blurring of outlines, the dissolution, the underwater effect, is much less marked than in the Chamber Concerto.

V. And it is most prominent, I think, in *Clocks and Clouds*.

L. Yes, there the well-delineated ticking effect is clearly separated from the blurred passages. The pattern is much simpler; *Clocks and Clouds* is one of my least complex compositions.

V. From the point of view of the musical material, there is no difference between the metronomic, ticking texture and the blurred one, the well-defined rhythmic movement and the cloudy dissolution, between the clocks and clouds.

L. I should like to refer to the soft, limp watches in Dali's painting (which had an associative value in the composition of this piece); the ticking clocks are transformed into clouds and then the clouds condense into ticking clocks.

V. Does it happen in any other of your compositions that the different types of musical movements are made up of the same musical material?

L. Not to the same extent as in *Clocks and Clouds*; in other works different types of music are not of the same homogeneous material. There the material is either completely homogeneous as in *Atmosphères*, where you find only one type of music, or there is very much contrast as in *Aventures*, the *Dies irae* of the Requiem and *Le Grand Macabre*.

V. Where does the title *Clocks and Clouds* come from?

L. It comes from Sir Karl Popper's 'Of Clouds and Clocks'.[8] I was interested in what he says about two kinds of processes in nature, one that you can measure exactly and the other which allows only for statistical approximation. The title is really the only feature my work and his essay have in common. It rather goes back to Krudy's clocks again. This reminds me of an

---

[8] The second Arthur Compton Memorial Lecture presented at Washington University on 21 April 1965. Published in *Objective Knowledge*, OUP, 1972.

interesting incident. I gave a long television interview on the BBC; they used a number of musical illustrations taken from recordings of my concerts. Speaking about *Clocks and Clouds* I mentioned Krudy's short story. Whereupon they went to Hungary and shot a number of clouds on the Great Plane to go with the music. I was astonished by the excellent visual associations the producer of the programme, Lesley Megahey, managed to create.

V.   Speaking about associations reminds me of those I had listening to the Double Concerto, chronologically your next work. In the second movement I had the impression that the rapidly moving music here is somehow static.

L.   Yes, this is an example of acoustic illusions, a favourite topic of mine. Something similar happens in *Continuum*; it is like the wheel of a railway engine, which at high speed seems stationary. Or think of the stroboscope effect, which was what you actually noticed in the second movement of the Double Concerto. Fast-moving music that seems static. It ties up again with the idea of something deep-frozen. Do you remember the prestissimo coda at the end of the work, when all the instruments play in a high register, re-creating the glittering sound of a glockenspiel or the piccolo and all that rapid movement is somehow frozen into motionlessness?

V.   We have discussed this idea of the deep-frozen effect in your music. Could you perhaps tell me what it is that makes you return again and again to this form of expression? What bell was sounded in you by Kleist, Kafka or Magritte?

L.   I could not tell you. Although it is something that often appears in my music I cannot tell you why I like it; I have never thought about it. Perhaps it is a form of defence, a way of overcoming fear; the fear of childhood fantasies or the very real fear of death I experienced in Nazi times. But I do not really know whether it goes back to past experiences.

V.   Perhaps it is in the air. In our times there have been plenty of reasons for it.

L.   All ages, or at least many ages have provided good reasons for it.

V.   Returning to your work, let us take the *San Francisco Polyphony*. I must confess first of all that I am not in such a good position to discuss this piece as the others; although I have a tape recording of it, I have never seen the score. So you will have to help me.

L.   There are two things in the title. It is an English title as it was commissioned by the San Francisco Symphony Orchestra and its first performance was in that city. The actual title is *Polyphony*. It is an orchestral work that is neither a symphony nor a concerto, so I simply called it *Polyphony*. It is a title that would really fit many of my compositions. In works like *Atmosphères* or *Lontano* the micropolyphony is not discernible, but from the Chamber Concerto onwards the tunes can be heard even if there are several of them played simultaneously blurring the sound.

In 1972 I stayed with my family at Stanford University for six months. Everybody knows that the situation of San Francisco is one of the most beautiful in the world; there California lives up to its reputation of 'eternal spring'. The city has a unique charm: it is not a very big place, a population of 700 to 750 thousand; its charm is partly due to its architecture. After the earthquake it was rebuilt in Victorian style; for the most part you find small English houses and the section with high-rise buildings is fairly small compared to other American cities. In originally laying out the plan for the city a great mistake was made, but it was an error that came to be one of San Francisco's attractions. They sent a map of the area – I think to Washington, where a regular, rectangular grid was drawn up for the streets. The planners had forgotten or did not know about the quite sizeable hills. The result is that some streets are so steep that it takes your breath away driving up and down them. There is just one winding road up a hill that was too precipitous and they decided to make an exception and not follow the plan as laid out in Washington. There are cable cars instead of trams. There is a groove between the rails and a steel cable pulls the car. The driver applies the brake by disconnecting a fork-like clamp. When he wants the car to start again he reconnects the clamp. There are always two cars together and it is not unlike trams in the summer used to be in Budapest, with open carriages. The cable car moves at such a slow speed that you can get on or off it while it is moving.

The various ethnic groups did not become integrated. San Francisco has the largest Chinese quarter outside East Asia, there are many Japanese, and in the Italian part of the city you would think you were in Italy. In addition to that there is the Californian attitude of ignoring conventions: you can go around in tails or fancy dress, if you like.

While I was working on *San Francisco Polyphony* I thought that the city's atmosphere had a decisive influence on the music, but when I heard it performed I realised it is more Viennese, there are a number of expressive melodies in it reminiscent of Alban Berg or Mahler. Only the end of the piece, the prestissimo section, with its machine-like, hectic quality makes you think of a big American city. But you must not think of it as programme music.

There is a lot of fog in San Francisco. In winter and summer thick fog spreads over the city from the Pacific a few hours before sunset. The fog covers half of the town and there it suddenly stops. The way it invades the town is impressive. Huge towering patches of fog move forward along the streets. Sometimes you can see enormous blobs of fog gliding under Golden Gate Bridge which is very high. It is a visual experience you only have on high mountains or in an aeroplane. You are sitting in full sunshine on the fiftieth floor of a building, in a café, and there is fog everywhere underneath. Here you have the idea of *Clocks and Clouds*. Tunes emerge from the fog and then sink back into it.

V.   I see that as I was preparing my notes I wrote the following sentence: melodic polyphony against a backdrop.

L.   Yes, the backdrop is the fog. As I mentioned earlier, this piece starts with a cluster full of various tunes that you cannot make out, as they are intertwined like creepers. Then slowly a very clear melodic pattern emerges from this dense texture, it is discernible for a while before it sinks back into the billowing mass. That is the overall structural principle of the work. Another characteristic feature is that the tunes are taken up by different instruments in turn and this produces different timbres.

V.   Now we come to your most recent major work, your opera, *Le Grand Macabre*. You have referred to it several times to illustrate various points. What interests me most is whether you also think that it marks a change in your style. I can find only a few passages that are characteristic of your earlier modes of expression and former structural patterns, the hectic, the static, the densely textured or the meccanico elements. Do you agree with me that the opera marks a stylistic change and, if so, is this change the logical outcome of your compositional development or did the genre impose the necessity of a new style?

L.   First of all, as far as stylistic change is concerned, there are in fact many elements in the opera that are characteristic of my earlier style, the hectic, wildly gesticulating elements. The coloratura arias essentially cover the whole of *Aventures*. But there is in fact a change of style. In *Le Grand Macabre* there is less of the static, slowly, gradually evolving music. I felt I had worn these types out. On the other hand, the multilayered quality we spoke about in connection with the Chamber Concerto figures prominently in the opera, for instance in the scene when Nekrotzar marches in. You must remember that twenty years of so-called avant-garde music, serial music, aleatory, timbre music, the post-Varèse school, Polish music, and not least my music; these are all things of the past. I myself have become part of that past. Therefore *Le Grand Macabre* marks almost as significant a change in my compositional development as my journey from Budapest to Cologne. I do not actually like to use the word development, I would rather say that I moved on in order to get somewhere new, as I did not want to repeat what I had already done earlier.

The younger generation of composers manifests a strong tendency for nostalgia, a return to romanticism, to tonality. But that is not for me. In all art forms, returning means running away. Just think of nineteenth-century Victorian architecture, breweries in Gothic style. That is out of the question for me. I am trying to do something different and this shows in *Le Grand Macabre*; you can also find it in the earlier *Pieces for Two Pianos*.
V.   What is different about it?
L.   That is difficult to put into words. Because if I say that, compared to my earlier works, tunes and clearly delineated rhythmic patterns have greater importance you could easily say that all this marks a return to an even earlier phase. You asked me if the genre dictates some stylistic change. Yes it does. *Aventures* was a kind of anti-opera, just like Kagel's immensely interesting *Staatstheater*. When I started work on the opera I meant to proceed along similar lines; then gradually I realised that the time of anti-operas is over. To use a witty phrase, I called *Le Grand Macabre* anti-anti-opera and the double negative results in an affirmation. *Le Grand Macabre* is an opera, after all. You can find the traditional operatic features in it. The influence of Monteverdi and Verdi is very clearly felt, in particular from the point of view of form. My opera does not have the continuous musical texture of Wagner operas nor is it divided into distinct periodic formal sections as is the case with Italian operas or Mozart. I have two models for it, Monteverdi's *Coronation of Poppea* and Verdi's *Falstaff*. A series of short episodes: orchestral intermezzi alternating with very short independent musical units. The overall form emerged from this episodic structure. But

I have been digressing again; I am supposed to say something about the style. The general stylistic features make up some kind of 'marché aux puces'; there is everything there; a traditional closing passacaglia, symphonic intermezzi, overture, fanfare, but everything is strangely transformed. It is half real, half unreal, a disintegrating, disorderly world where everything is falling in, breaking up. The overture is modelled on the opening fanfares of Monteverdi's *Orfeo*. It is not a quotation, the similarity is one of general character. In place of the wind instruments I have twelve old-fashioned car klaxons with the rubber balls to sound them. These klaxons stand in for the brass, they are brass instruments gone all wrong, symbolizing the general atmosphere of dilapidation and ruin. There are tonal passages, atonal ones, many quotations from music of past ages. All these go into my marché aux puces. When you are in the middle of it with all the stalls and wares and shouting around you, such a market is the very essence of disorder, but watching it from above, from a balcony, all the pieces make up a unit, a single vast pattern. That is how I see both form and style in *Le Grand Macabre*. You remember the old Weiner story. When at a dinner party old uncle Leo dropped a piece of paté on the floor he smeared and pressed it into the carpet with the sole of his shoes, so that people would not notice. That is something like what I did. I squeezed all the scraps of the history of music into the opera.

V. Are the quotations, both musical and scenic, in fact parodies?

L. Taken on the whole the opera is both a parody and it is serious. What is time all about? Death appears, Doomsday has come. But Death turns out to be not a real person but some confused Don Quixote. (Sancho Panza is there too with him in the person of Piet, the realist, who is at the same time Rosinante; Don Quixote rides on him.) You may consider sections of the music parodies or you may not. Take the scene when Nekrotzar marches on to the stage. All through this passage you can hear, as an ostinato in the bass, the bass subject in the finale of Beethoven's *Eroica* Symphony, but it is transformed into twelve-note music, not quite twelve-note music, there are thirteen notes. It is a parody to start with but the music becomes in the end quite serious and dignified. And this applies to the whole opera; fragments of parody are pressed into the musical texture.

V. I think that the final conclusion of the opera, the last lines, 'Death will come some day, but not yet, and until then let us be merry' is something that you can take seriously.

L. If you listen to the music carefully you find it not only serious but also somehow very sad. We are alive, *carpe diem*, let us make the best of our allotted time; yet there is nothing hedonistic about it.

V. That is a question I wanted to ask. What is the reason for the contrast between the text and the rather dry quality of the final passacaglia? Such a contrast does not seem to follow from your interpretation of the last scene.

L. The text of the opera is both serious and comical. The whole situation is humorous. A couple come on who had been making love all through the alleged end of the world, they are tired, they do not want to hear about the end of the world. Death has died. If he really was Death then we shall live for ever. If, however, Nekrotzar was not really Death then everything goes on as before. The key statement is made by Piet, always a realist. He thinks he has got to heaven, but everything seems the same as on earth, what is the point of dying? Everything is the same as before, Doomsday or no Doomsday.

V. Is that the reason for the qualilty of the final passacaglia? I find the music slightly dry; not contrived, just simply dry.

L. But there is something I should add here. The opera as a whole tends to this. The passacaglia is the only section of the opera that is wholly consonant. The bass subject consists of twelve minor and twelve major sixths, one major and one minor sixth for all twelve notes of the chromatic scale. The resulting twenty-four intervals do not make up a real bass subject, they serve as a frame, which is filled up by major and minor thirds. Consequently, you get major and minor chords. All are consonant chords, sweet, almost syrupy, but it is not tonal music. You are quite right that here the honied quality of this passage becomes dry, partly through the orchestration (an almost Stravinsky-like orchestration) and partly through the short duration of the individual notes. It is another application of the freezing technique. My answer to whether it is all parody is that it both is and is not. The various connotations have been pressed into the carpet too.

V. And that is another example of the dualism in your work. Coming to the end of this discussion about your works, how about these lines of Kosztolányi as a motto: 'Blessed is he who brings the new; the new that is old but new to our eyes'?

L. Very beautiful lines.

70

V.   Do you agree that they apply to you?
L.   Yes, absolutely.

III

V.   In our first conversation we tried to give a general picture, in the second we went through your output to date in chronological order. For the last conversation I suggest the title: György Ligeti, musician.

You have been teaching at the Hamburg conservatory since 1973. Could you tell me something about your educational ideas, or if you like, about your praxis, your practical work as a teacher.
L.   Praxis is a good word for it, it is an exercise. I am constitutionally an anti-educationalist, and in any case you cannot teach composition. You can teach the technical aspects of it, harmony, musical form, counterpoint, orchestration. My requirement is that everybody that intends to compose what you call modern music – any kind of modern music – should be perfectly familiar with tertian harmony, Palestrina and Bach counterpoint, should be able to write fugues and should be conversant with musical forms. This is an indispensable knowledge even if as a composer he will not use it. That was my conclusion after studying with Ferenc Farkas, and also with Sándor Veress, Kadosa and Járdányi. I was lucky to have had the opportunity to learn all the rules of traditional musical technique. They served me more than I can say, in everything I did, be it micro-polyphony, multilayered textures or anything else. Without the Palestrina exercises I learned through Jeppesen I would never have been able to work out intricate micropolyphonic textures. I would swear by the importance of traditional techniques. But there is also a negative side to studying composition. Whereas I find it extremely important to learn how to handle sonata form or rondo form, I am totally against the use of traditional forms for present-day melodic, harmonic or rhythmic material. Knowing how to analyse traditional forms is indispensable but God save us from atonal sonatas.

Teaching a composition class all you can do is to go through the scores of your students, criticize them, discuss problems of technique and particularly of orchestration, point out if there are any discrepancies in the musical material. It took me some time to realise this. My class in Hamburg was not my first experience in teaching composition. From the early '60s I had been teaching several weeks every year, first in Stockholm and then in California. In Stockholm I was standing in for Karl-Birger Blomdahl. He maintained a very high standard. His syllabus included not only Jeppesen and Hindemith's *Unterweisung im Tonsatz* but also some techniques of serial and twelve-note music. I did not quite agree with his teaching twelve-note technique, which by the early '60s had become past history and taken its place alongside Bach's or Palestrina's counterpoint. I tried to find some new ideas, for instance, the handling of timbre. I composed exercise pieces in one part or just on one note where the form emerged from the changes of timbre. I said I was opposed to composition exercises, but if the examples I have quoted surely contradict this, the explanation is that my attitude has radically changed since then. Now I would not think of practising such methods in teaching.

V.   You are, in effect, not giving a class but conducting a master-class.

L.   It is not called that but it really amounts to that. In my class in Hamburg everybody is a trained composer. What matters is not whether they have a diploma but whether they have gone through all the traditional studies, harmony, counterpoint, musical forms. The only area where I give actual classes is in Bach's counterpoint. Most academies do not maintain a sufficiently high standard in teaching it. At the moment one of my assistants takes this class; earlier I had tortured him with inventions and fugues for two years. That leaves me more time for conducting the free composition class. There are eight young composers in my class; we meet twice a week for a whole afternoon. I do not teach them individually; in fact we have a free discussion – you could almost call it a high level café conversation. All of them have reached the standard of being able to judge a composition by looking at the score, but we play it on the piano if we have the chance. During the discussion everybody points out what he likes or does not like from the point of view of style, etc. As all eight of them are fully trained composers most of the works under discussion have already been performed or are shortly going to be performed, and sooner or later we can listen to all the works from a tape recording. I take great pains with orchestration. Although I am not dogmatic about principles, I require an orchestration that is adequate for each work. By adequate I mean it should either clearly mark certain elements or, in fact, blur them completely.

72

Rimsky-Korsakov's textbook on orchestration is a prescribed book and so is the Kunitz, which in my opinion is the most detailed study of all in the use of instruments in an orchestral score.

That is one of my tasks in Hamburg. I also give a class that anybody can attend. There are usually twenty-five to thirty-five people, some from the Academy, some from other places, from the University for instance. It is a class in musical analysis. I choose a new subject for every half-year semester. For two semesters we analysed Webern's works, then devoted three semesters to the late Schubert, Mahler, Debussy. The subject of the next semester is Mozart's style. We shall try to define the elements in Mozart that distinguish his style from that of Haydn, of the Mannheim School or of J.C. Bach – what makes it typically Mozart. The essence does not really emerge from the analysis, but you can pinpoint technical questions such as the importance of some types of melody, figure, ornament, of a sudden chromatic transition, and find the constituents of that incredible balance in Mozart's music. We shall go through his highly chromatic works (G-minor Quintet, G-minor Symphony) and his extraordinarily rich pieces in the major key (*Così fan tutte*) from this point of view. The course is really a seminar. I am not the only one to speak; one or other of the participants tells us about a subject and we discuss it. I try to keep the standard as high as possible, so that I must say quite a lot of people drop out. The ideal I follow here is Lajos Bárdos, the way he conducted his analysis classes.

V. What are the ideas of the younger composers, as far as you can see; any new trends, tendencies? The kind of neo-romantic, neo-tonal music you have mentioned earlier?

L. This is a very strong tendency in Germany. Although Western European countries maintain a certain cultural homogeneity, the trends vary from country to country. The prevailing international musical style of the '50s and '60s has given way now to a differentiation of musical style along linguistic dividing lines. In German-speaking countries neo-tonality is in fashion, nostalgic music, but you find hardly any trace of it in France. Young French composers follow Boulez or Xenakis; one group of composers there adopted the technique used in my *Atmosphères*, with a time lag of fifteen to twenty years. In America general fashions used to change every two to three years; now there is a trend that is the equivalent to photorealism in the visual arts. Some composers write nineteenth-century music without any distancing, for instance, a Schumann song, which I find foolish.

V. And the same in Germany?

L. No, the German nostalgic trend is more serious. Their return to tonality is marked by an alienated quality. It is not photorealism but rather reminiscent of the 'plush' features of Mahler and Strauss. What they are doing is original; they all agree in rejecting the Cologne-Darmstadt avant-garde. But their rejection means a return to an earlier musical style.

V. Has this trend been initiated by young composers or do they follow some important and well-known composer?

L. It is entirely the initiative of younger composers. As for me, I do not want to interfere in any way in questions of style – standard and quality is what interests me – but I do not approve of any 'neo' trend. I have heated discussions with my students about questions of style. Several young composers who follow the trend are in my class, so many people believe that it is all my influence, but I categorically deny any such allegation.

V. What is behind this trend?

L. I think it is partly due to musical and partly to extraneous reasons. You could sum up the musical considerations as follows: they are fed up with serial music, with aleatory music, with Cage's Dadaism, with everything you used to hear and can still hear in Darmstadt. All this has worn thin during the past twenty years. I share this feeling; the subject arose last time when we were talking about *Le Grand Macabre*. I quite approve of the complete rejection of the past twenty years on the part of the young composers. It is a healthy sign. However, I remain sceptical. It is all right rejecting what is past, but they should do something genuinely new, instead of returning to late Romantic, pathos-filled German music.

V. Perhaps Stravinsky will turn out to be right, in what he said in his *Conversations with Robert Craft* about the music of the future: some people will attach a slide ruler to their score but Rachmaninov will be the general taste, all in high-fidelity production.

L. That is a big subject to discuss. I do not think it will be quite like that. You find high-fidelity Rachmaninov in the works of the American photorealists, who project Schumann onto their manuscripts, well no, Schumann is of a rather high standard, let us leave it at Rachmaninov. The young German group of composers are on a much higher level both in taste and in what they want to express. Their music is expressive, it streams with pathos and passion. I think that on the one hand they are reacting to the avant-garde of the past thirty years but that they also put on a fancy dress of old, nineteenth-century cut.

V. Is that what you meant by extraneous reasons?

L. No, that was something else. I know that dividing periods into decades is vague and does not really fit, but it is rather handy for practical purposes. A typical feature of the '60s was colourfulness: the discovery of *fin de siècle* taste, of ornaments; that was the time of the flower power, of hippies. In music it marked a reaction to serial music or its fine art equivalent, op-art. All this colour brought with it in Western Europe some kind of free and easy mentality in the '60s. Since 1972, or 1973, since the oil crisis, the '70s brought another change in mentality. The colourful, hippy mentality is still with us but is much less significant. The soul has gone out of Happenings and of Cage's principle about the identity of life and art. We live in a different world that is difficult to define as it is too close to us. I could describe it as conformism; it applies not only to music but to everything else.

V. Was the year of change perhaps 1968 rather than 1972, the Paris of 1968?

L. I think 1968 was still essentially part of the hippy movement, whose influence was felt until the early '70s. Music in those years was colourful, whereas today it is grey. Since the mid-'70s conformism has been very much in the air, in any case in Germany, Austria, England and the Scandinavian countries I am more familiar with. The young want security. You could almost say that they want to go on pension as soon as they leave secondary school; well, I am exaggerating. It may be the voice of an adult judging the young harshly and unjustly, but I can sense a desire for security; the new musical trend we have talked about is a manifestation of the same tendency. Back to the nineteenth century, it is safe, let us stop experimenting, you can almost hear them say. Since such a lot happened between 1900 and 1978 I am rather suspicious of such an unthoughtful striving for the past.

V. We are not qualified to prophesy, I know, but I wonder whether a more complex trend, the way you put it, has any future?

L. That you will only be able to tell when the whole matter has become past history. Who knows, some genius may appear from the new groups and create something extraordinary. It may be due to our mentality; for our generation, progress is enormously important and we find there is a contradiction between progress and a return to the past. I have a strong urge to go forward, but I may be wrong. Perhaps I am an old fuddy-duddy who has failed to grasp the spirit of the age. We had better refrain from prophecies, for they are subjective, they spring from our desires. You can see in history that nothing happened in the way people imagined. The same applies to the arts. We simply do not know.

V.   Talking about the nineteenth century gives me the opportunity to go on to my next point. You said in a letter: I like all good music. I should now like to ask you questions about the music of former times. We have spoken about several composers but only from the viewpoint of their influencing your work and in what way. I should like to ask your opinion about some other composers – I will mention names at random, without regard to any chronological order. First of all someone who has appeared several times during our conversation: Gustav Mahler, whom we both like so much. What features of his music do you appreciate most, in what way do you find him an outstanding composer?

L.   His orchestration, which may seem a secondary feature but is not. The way he handled the orchestra, allowing one instrument to play *fortissimo* while at the same time another is marked *pianissimo*. A flute played *pianissimo* in the high register for instance would cut through low register strings played *fortissimo*. Before Mahler, orchestrating an accent meant all the instruments stressing the same note to the same degree. The simultaneous multi-layered treatment of accent was an innovation of Mahler and Stravinsky; they introduced a much more differentiated treatment of accent. That is one aspect of my appreciation. The other is a consideration of form. I particularly like those interminably long movements such as the finale of the Sixth Symphony and the first movements of the Third and Ninth. All three have the general shape of a sonata rondo, but to conceive of them in that way is really meaningless. The form rolls on like an epic narrative. Adorno called it a novel in sound: a very good observation. Another reason why I like Mahler so much is this: it was not until fairly late in life that I got to know his music. I was an adult then. Around 1947 when I was a student in Budapest I heard two magnificent concerts, Klemperer conducting Mahler's Fourth Symphony and the First Symphony with Kleiber; the latter was the most momentous experience I have ever had listening to a conductor. It was not Mahler that impressed me – in

76

those days I did not particularly like his music; I considered him one of those bombastic late Romantic composers whose works are filled with pathos: it was a world alien to me. It was not just that I, personally, did not like it, the prevailing atmosphere was against it, you were not supposed to like him.

V. Don't you think that we ought to forget everything we learned back in those days in the way of musical appreciation?

L. Well, I think that Bence Szabolcsi's Mozart analysis still holds good, although many things we used not to like then appear in a very different light now, thirty years later. Mahler was a taste I acquired later. I have spent most of my time in Vienna in the past twenty years, which may have contributed to my getting to like Mahler; the Viennese aura has captured me. But it did not do as much where Schoenberg is concerned, although he was also a Viennese. I respect him, consider him significant, I like some of his works but I am simply not in sympathy with the somewhat academic, post-Brahmsian character of his music. The will to greatness in Schoenberg's music somehow lacks credibility much as it is credible in the case of Beethoven.

V. What about Mahler?

L. The ambition in Mahler is such a wonderful failure. His ambitious overall forms somehow always fail; it is really touching. You find in his music a gap between the symphonic aspirations and the result, which came in for very harsh criticism at the time. The opinion was that his music tends to disintegration. The apparent lack of logic in his forms was not understood, whereas I am particularly attracted by that rent quality, his 'Zerrissenheit'. Mahler is a composer you can both admire and feel compassion for at the same time.

The same will to greatness in Wagner, Richard Strauss and Schoenberg leaves me cold; but I approve of it in the case of Berg. And I like Webern's striving for the small.

V. What do you exactly mean by will to greatness?

L. Pompousness among other things. It is the same as someone who wants to do something big, build the tallest tower, compose the longest, the biggest symphony. Think of Berlioz. The *Symphonie funèbre et triomphale* needs thousands of performers; such an ostentatious gesture is something I utterly dislike. I am much more attuned to the 'great music through small means', to Mozart's way. But when the will to greatness does realize its ambition, as in the first movement of Beethoven's Fifth Symphony, that is overwhelmingly wonderful. I also recognize

Wagner's greatness but I do not really like his music. All these are personal, subjective opinions.

V. That is what I really want to hear.

L. If you ask me who are my favourite composers I should have to confess that my opinion is in a state of change. In the '60s I was very interested in Mahler. But I would not put him on the highest pedestal, I do not think he ranks with the greatest.

V. Who would you put there?

L. First of all the same four composers as everyone else, Bach, Mozart, Beethoven and Schubert. Next comes, at the moment, Schumann; I have always liked Schumann but now he is particularly significant for me. I am trying to change the course of my music, give up the completely cool, distanced music, or rather a music that is as if observed from afar; I want to get it closer to the current, give it immediacy, and in this Schumann's influence on me is considerable.

V. The four great composers do not need any further comment. What attracts you to Schumann? I mean in strictly musical, technical terms.

L. Technically speaking I am fascinated by Schumann's internal ornamentation. In his piano music, you always find meandering lines embedded in the texture. There was nothing like that before him. Another point is his formal structure. You find the conventional overall formal patterns but these are not what really matter. Within the overall structure and on a more delicate level everything is urging forward.

It is quite unlike the static, balanced form of the Viennese classics and of the less balanced Schubert. Schumann's internal weaving of lines, both very dense and unsystematic, is not really contrapuntal, it consists in figures and ornaments run wild. It is very original, and in some ways profoundly affects the development of his formal structures. It gives the impression of a musical form that has overflown the banks.

V. Your being an operatic composer prompts the question, what is your opinion about Mozart and Verdi operas?

L. It is a commonplace that *Don Giovanni* and *Figaro* are the most magnificent operas ever written and *Così fan tutte* the most beautiful music there is. I should not say that Mozart was my ideal; the comparison is unseemly. Anyway, his non-literary operas were my models, the way he brings characters' personalities and situations to life through music. In the realm of musical drama I consider the late Verdi almost on the same level.

Falstaff's character is depicted in musical terms although Boito's libretto is also quite admirable. You could say that Falstaff's very pot-belly is delineated by the musical texture. But that is also a commonplace.

V. What is not yet commonplace and what you also may eventually come round to is that *Falstaff* is not the only masterpiece in Verdi's output?

L. I am stressing this because for *Le Grand Macabre* opera buffa of that kind was my model. Ever since a child I have been a Verdi fan. I like *Otello* and also Verdi's middle period almost as much as *Falstaff*.

V. May I mention another composer who usually tends to be a controversial issue when I talk to composers? During our conversation you made a rather derogatory remark about Puccini.

L. His sentimentality is very alien to me but I like the second act of *La Bohème*, the complexity of its musical texture; different dramatic layers interlace here with one another to form a wonderful simultaneity. Apart from *La Bohème*, *Gianni Schicchi* is not bad. But I cannot stand *Tosca* or *Turandot*.

V. Don't you think that it may be a matter of how it is performed, in what style?

L. It may be. I am always ready to change my mind. I have often done so in the past and sometimes quite radically. Sometimes I like a composer although I do not like some of his works. Debussy is one of my real favourites. *Pelléas* is wonderful music but as a dramatic work it is tedious. I would never go to see it however marvellous the production. There are works that I will never like. *Parsifal* will always remain unbearable for me and I detest *Rosenkavalier*.

V. May I go back to Mahler, to consider just one more point, which links up with the last subject we are going to talk about. Do you think that part of the reason why Mahler wanted to create something big was that for him a symphony, how should I put it, was a pulpit from which he could address the whole of humanity? Which would make him share a Wagnerian ambition?

L. You refer to the ideological side of him, to his conviction that music is not just music but a message. I hate missionaries, missions of any creed, of science too, whose missionaries are all pseudo-scientific, anyway.

V. That is what I was driving at. Instead of mission perhaps we should stick to the word message. Does music have a message for humanity, the audience, the public – to put it in this pompous fashion. And the next logical question, has your music got a message?

L.   Oh yes, that is a fashionable question.

V.   Well, it has been fashionable ever since the first work was composed.

L.   I do not think that anybody would have thought of asking such a question in Bach's, Haydn's or Mozart's time. People make music, they would have said. Message – they would not have understood what that question meant. This whole problem, I think, arose with the musical 'Titans' of the late nineteenth century. Why do I compose? Quite frankly I compose music because I feel like it. For myself, without feeling I have any mission to fulfil. I know the next cross-question is going to be whether I would compose music on a desert island, knowing that my works would never be performed. That, I do not know. As I said, I compose for myself but it makes me feel very good if other people like my music, if they speak well of it. As for changing the world or saving it, changing people, or advocating the 'true creed' . . .

V.   None of these things, but music may just be like an acknowledgement.

L.   Yes, but it should not be consciously that. No doubt all compositions convey somehow all the experience the composer has accumulated, what you could call his attitude to life. That cannot be helped. But it is quite another matter to advertise it, saying 'that is the message I bring'; no, that is not for me. I write music as I like, but of course it is also there for anybody who wants to listen to it. I would not make compromises to be popular. That is what I meant when I said I would not write music for home use – I do not mean Haydn Quartets or Schubert's piano works for four hands, but music with an educational slant. I approve of the educational value of *Mikrokosmos*, it is a form of technical training. What I feel quite alien to me is, to turn the phrase round, big hands, small masters.

V.   Just now I thought I had almost managed to corner you. Wouldn't you go back there?

L.   Willingly, but where is the corner?

V.   The corner is the purpose of music: the acknowledgement, the experience, the attitude to life. One of my first questions was: does life affect the work? Your answer was entirely affirmative.

L.   It does, indirectly. It is not as if when you are sad you

80

compose sad music. It would be quite wrong to say that. While working on a composition it never occurs to me whether people will like it, how it will be received. But I am in the same position as the next man, living at a certain period, in a particular social context; whether I want it or not other people will always find in my music something they understand. I have not adopted some hermetic language, even though the musical language I use may seem difficult to make out at first – you need a trained ear to understand it right away. In brief, I write music for myself but it is bound to convey something to others; that is all I can say about your message. My message is not a deliberate programme but an indirect, implied message that is present in all music.

V.   To return to my favourite image. Sit on the chandelier, look down at yourself. What was the message you spoke about just now? Now we are back in the corner.

L.   Well, that is not easy to put into words but I will try to look at my overall work from afar, as if I had nothing to do with it. I am reminded of something that has already come up in our conversations: fear and overcoming fear by distancing yourself from it. Look at fear from the wrong side of the telescope. That may be a basic feature of my music, but not its message. The comic elements, fear, buffa and seria are not only inextricably mixed up in it, they merge and become one and the same thing. What is serious is at the same time comical and the comical is terrifying. Viewing my output from a distant vantage point, that is what I could find genuinely new in it, something that has not been done in this way before; the two *Aventures*, *Le Grand Macabre*. By the way, I have seen two productions of my opera. One production made it demoniac and although in many respects I found the production unsatisfactory, of the two, I found this one right. The other production was more streamlined, had more verve but it gave a disproportionate emphasis to the comic aspect, reducing the demoniac element to a minimum. A more accomplished production but less satisfactory.

V.   Could we make a high-level generalization? Let the public be there in place of the producer and György Ligeti's entire output in place of *Le Grand Macabre*, would what you have just said still apply?

L.   Yes, I think so.

V.   We have got there.

L.   Am I back in the corner?

V.   No, not any longer. The correct way of putting it could be;

the message is the act of acknowledging our time.

L.   It is all in there whether you want it or not.

V.   May I turn it around? Not that it is in there, but that is what is essentially there.

L.   Maybe.

(1978)   *Translation from Hungarian by Gabor J. Schabert*

2

LIGETI – JOSEF HÄUSLER

I

Two days before the première of the orchestral work, Lontano– *the recording had already been made – I had an appointment with György Ligeti to record a conversation with him for the Südwestfunk [South West German Radio]. I was actually thinking of nothing more than an introduction to* Lontano *in the form of an interview; nevertheless, we had not stipulated how the conversation should proceed, nor how long it should last, and since we were both improvising, the whole thing suddenly took a different direction. The fifteen to twenty minutes we had envisaged turned into nearly two hours of talk which, when it had been tidied up somewhat and musical examples added, yielded two Südwestfunk broadcasts.[1] They were called 'From* Atmosphères *to* Lontano'. *At first, obviously, it was not intended to publish them in print. As this possibility then arose, it proved necessary to edit the text in certain particulars, condensing it in various places, while endeavouring not to affect its character of an improvised conversation. The [original] publisher and the editor wish to thank György Ligeti not only for his permission to go into print, but also for taking part in this editing.*

Josef Häusler

Häusler: Mr Ligeti, in a commentary to your orchestral work, *Lontano*, you wrote: 'There is not just one single harmonic form process, but several simultaneous processes with different speeds which glimmer through, superimpose themselves on one another and produce an imaginary perspective through all sorts of refraction and reflection. It reveals itself gradually to the listener, as though he were going into a dark room from bright sunlight and little by little becoming aware of the colours and contours.'

[1] Broadcast by the Südwestfunk, Baden-Baden, on 19 and 26 July 1968

83

I find myself in this position, and should be grateful if you would help me and the people listening to us to perceive the colours and contours more precisely. Perhaps, to begin with, I could simply ask you a question: how is *Lontano* different from your earlier works, and what connects it to these works?

Ligeti: I should like to talk first about the question of similarity. *Lontano* and a few earlier works such as *Atmosphères*, *Apparitions*, or a work which came just before *Lontano*, the Cello Concerto – particularly the first movement of the Cello Concerto – the organ work *Volumina*, and the second movement from the Requiem – the *Kyrie* movement – these all have something in common, viz., the way in which the music appears. I do not mean by that the 'musical form'; the musical form can be structured very differently, but I mean a kind of musical aura. It is music that gives the impression that it could stream on continuously, as if it had no beginning and no end; what we hear is actually a section of something that has eternally begun and that will continue to sound for ever. It is typical of all these pieces that there are hardly any caesuras and the music really does flow on. The formal characteristic of this music is that it seems static. The music appears to stand still, but that is merely an illusion: within this standing still, this static quality, there are gradual changes: I would think here of a surface of water in which an image is reflected; then this surface of water is gradually disturbed, and the image disappears, but very, very gradually. Subsequently the water calms down again, and we see a different image. That is, of course, merely a metaphor or association, but one can see metaphorical elements even in the titles of these works. Typical of this is *Atmosphères*, where the word 'atmosphere' itself has a dual meaning: atmosphere in the literal sense of the word and also in the figurative sense. I would say that the music has a kind of metaphorical relationship to both senses of the word, in a similar way to the titles of the 'Préludes' used by Debussy. In the score, Debussy put the titles not at the beginning but at the end of each piece, in brackets. This way of presenting titles – one can also find something similar in the realm of painting, with Paul Klee, who usually named his paintings and drawings later – is rather like mine: it's not an external thing, it belongs, as it were, to the conception of this kind of music. And to come back to *Atmosphères*: it has something atmospheric, that is to say, something floating, indeterminate, almost contourless, merging into itself, and on the other hand, something atmospheric in the figurative sense. I should like to hope, or believe that I could, that the work, even if it is not exactly expressive, nevertheless has a quite definite feeling or emotion about it, and that is precisely what is atmospheric or *ambience*-like. Yes, I don't think that one can say any more about it.

H.   I think it is time to play an extract from *Atmosphères* for our listeners, so that they can have an idea of the tonal picture of this work.

L.   Yes, I would suggest a passage from the middle of the work, where after a deep, low-lying, bunched-up double-bass – I won't say exactly 'chord', but a chromatically filled complex, a kind of tone-cluster – the strings come in almost inaudibly, that is, the remaining strings, the whole orchestra of strings dismantles into individual voices; there are altogether fifty-six voices in the strings and yet one hardly hears this entrance. It comes very softly, still somewhat hidden by the double-basses, and then gradually the double-basses disappear, and the remaining strings, joined later by the double-basses playing *pianissimo*, take over the very soft movement of the individual voices. This passage could be taken as typical for the whole aura of the music. The voices, considered individually, have a very specific channelling, are each composed separately, in their own right. In combination they yield a contrapuntal structure. If one analyses the work from the score, one can see a kind of canon technique, but one cannot hear it, for a canon with so many voices – it has first forty-eight and then later fifty-six – is no longer heard as a canon; instead, we hear a continuous musical web ('web' being used here purely as a metaphor), and the music seems to spin itself out without any incisions. In this example, the following happens: at the entrance of the strings, the breadth of the plane of sound (*Klangfläche*) which is then mobile within itself, is determined by the contra-puntal internal structure; the plane of sound is wide: that is to say, it stretches from the lowest to the highest register and is fairly uniformly spaced out chromatically. I say, 'fairly uniformly'. If I said uniformly, that would mean that all the chromatic intervals are there. This is not the case. There are small gaps, because the parts are constantly changing, and so there are places where notes are doubled, but where other notes are missing. So you get a kind of tonal iridescence. This iridescence is further completed by the fact that gradually different kinds of bowing can be heard; it begins *sul tasto*, then goes into normal bowing, then into *sul ponticello*, and finally at a crescendo it returns to normal bowing.

85

Hand in hand with this transformation of tone-colour and dynamics, there is a compression of the plane of sound: that is to say, it gets narrower and narrower, almost as if it were being crammed into a funnel (I am possibly speaking in too concrete terms now, but I don't mean to as regards the music). This funnel becomes narrower and narrower until it is a kind of whirlpool or vortex; if one looks at the score, one finds that the music turns in two directions, almost like a cyclone and an anti-cyclone; the high strings have a definite direction in their scoring, and the violas, cellos and double-basses have exactly the opposite. These two directions are finally united, overlapping each other or growing into one another to such an extent that the two different movements can no longer be heard, and the big plane of sound is narrowed from an expanse of several octaves down to a minor third – from the lower B flat to the middle D flat. The third is chromatically spaced, but again with constant movement. One could say that this passage from *Atmosphères* is typical of the thought behind continuous processes, typical of a formal trans-formation that depends most of all on the changing tone-colours. I should like to emphasize that point most strongly, for *Atmos-phères* is a composition in tone-colours *par excellence* and is closely connected with Schoenberg's third orchestral piece from his opus 16. In recent works, however, in the Cello Concerto, or especially in *Lontano* or in the choral work *Lux aeterna*, although I work formally in a similar fashion the tone-colours no longer have predominance in articulating the form.

Musical excerpt from Atmosphères: *bar 44 (letter H) to bar 53 (letter L)*

H. Let me return once more to your commentary on *Lontano*. You write there the lapidary sentence: 'Polyphony is written, but harmony is heard.' We have heard a passage from *Atmosphères* that represents, at least in part, a kind of 56-voice canon, and one could perhaps paraphrase your quotation by saying: 'Polyphony is written, but tone-colour or plane of sound is heard.' Before we come to talk about *Lontano*, just one little digression. This iridescence of the planes of sound, this dovetailing into each other, dissolving away from each other, the alternation of types of sound – from the sound of woodwind to the sound of brass, from the sound of brass to the sound of strings, and so on – may occasionally remind us of different kinds of noise-colours in electronics. Do electronics, or electronic sound concepts play a

86

role in your music?

L. Certainly, an important role, and I've also dabbled in electronic music . . .

H. Yes, you created the work *Artikulation* in the studio of the Westdeutscher Rundfunk [West German Radio] in Cologne . . .

L. Yes, and two other pieces which, however, are private, which I regard as finger exercises, as it were. I am often asked the question whether my orchestral works *Atmosphères* and *Apparitions* are not rather electronic music played by an orchestra. Many listeners who have heard the works only on tape, have asked me whether it was not just a question of manipulating tapes, and I have always answered, 'No, nothing at all has been manipulated, there is nothing electronic in it at all, nor are there many unusual methods of playing the instruments. I do not want to say that there aren't any at all: there are certain methods of playing that are innovatory . . .'

H. Perhaps you are thinking of the place where the piano's strings are rubbed with cloths and brushes?

L. Yes, or similar things, like having only air in the brass instruments: that happened at the end of *Apparitions*; or I think of quite definite, innovatory pizzicati that I tried out, mostly in *Apparitions*, or of certain sections in which the strings play a kind of harmonic but on parts of the string where there is no nodal point for a harmonic. Then you don't get the sound of a harmonic, but rather something noisy: I would say something between sound and noise.

H. I believe, Mr Ligeti, we should now play that for our listeners. Shall we perhaps choose the place from *Atmosphères* where the piano is rubbed with cloths and brushes – just before the end, if I'm not mistaken?

L. Yes, that is just as the music begins to fade: you can hear that very clearly there. The rubbing with the brushes begins while the orchestra is still playing, namely all the strings and in addition the trombones with deep pedal notes. Finally the strings and then the trombones are silent and one is left – as a kind of echo of the trombones – with only this friction of the lower piano notes. I must quickly add here that technically that wasn't my invention: it was to be found earlier in music written by certain composers for films, and we don't really know who invented all that. I think also of Cage, who has prepared the piano in every possible kind of way, but the question of who did it first doesn't really need to be asked. I adopted it, not for effect, but because I was looking for a particular sound that produces an organic and apparently sustained continuation, a kind of pedal effect for the whole orchestra. This and other special instrumental effects were chosen only because they belonged to the musical conception.

Musical excerpt: Atmosphères, *bar 59 (letter M) to the end*

H. Let me question you further: it is therefore not a case of electronic manipulations; yet the conception of sound behind your *Atmosphères* is connected somehow with the concept of sound in electronic music – or would you consider that beside the point?

L. No, no, most certainly not. Not only is there a point of connection, but there are several of different kinds. First of all, my practical experience in the studio of the Westdeutscher Rundfunk[2] where I learned a great deal from Stockhausen, Eimert and Koenig. All this naturally had an effect on my later instrumental music. For this reason, in *Apparitions* and *Atmosphères* – those were the first two instrumental pieces after my work in the electronic studio – there are certain sounds or sound transformations that would not have occurred otherwise. Perhaps I would still have composed them, but not in this form. So that was, as I said, the influence of working in the electronic studio. But I can turn the question round: I already had concepts of static planes of sound that gradually alter, before I had ever heard any electronic music...

H. ... and did you also have these concepts before you came to Western Europe in 1956? Did they occur to you while you were still in Budapest?

L. Yes. I can tell you exactly: they date from 1950. Up to then, and even a little later, my compositions were largely influenced by Bartók and Stravinsky, and to a certain extent by Alban Berg. They were the three modern composers I knew well. Yes, and I knew Hindemith well, too, but was less influenced by him. Schoenberg and Webern, however, I scarcely knew at all. I would say, Schoenberg only a little and Webern not at all. For example, I wrote a string quartet in 1953 to 1954, *Métamorphoses nocturnes*, that was influenced not only by Bartók but also by Alban Berg's *Lyric Suite*. I only had the score, and hadn't actually heard any of Berg's works, but the score impressed me a great deal. Well, in 1950 I suddenly realised that I could no longer model my work on Bartók or Stravinsky. I was then twenty-seven

[2] West German Radio – Cologne

years old, I had already composed a lot, and was dissatisfied with all of it. In addition, one has to know about the peculiar situation in Hungary, and in Eastern Europe altogether at the beginning of the '50s. We were totally isolated from all the musical developments in Western Europe. By chance, I happened to hear a few programmes broadcast at night by the Bayrischer Rundfunk,[3] the Südwestfunk,[4] the WDR[5] and the NDR;[6] but these were very curious impressions, since the German broadcasting stations, and all those in the West, suffered from a great deal of jamming: with a view to jamming not the music, but the news broadcasts. So it was with these programmes at night. Besides that, one never knew exactly when they were going to take place, as there were no radio magazines available. So at about 11 o'clock, one started excitedly trying to find something: between 11 and 12 o'clock there was always contemporary music. I heard, for example, pieces by Messiaen, Fortner, and also by Boulez, Stockhausen, Nono and many others, but usually only the very high notes – everything else disappeared under the crackle. This was hardly very informative. I would say that one learned about Western music more from hear-say. There was a time immediately after the war when one could get periodicals – *Melos*, for example – but one couldn't hear the music.

So I came to realise that it was of no interest whatsoever to continue composing in the manner of Bartók, even if I wrote music as advanced as, for example, Bartók in the string quartets of his middle period – although mine would of course be technically much more primitive. I didn't yet have this technical ability. But even works like that were composed only to be put away in a drawer. One could not perform that sort of thing. If someone like myself did not follow the political line of the day, then they were forced to stick to simpler educational works and arrangements of folk-songs. I did a lot in this field, which I didn't regard as a compromise. That was the situation at the time in Hungary. Then there was an internal opposition, as it were, which consisted in concentrating on Stravinsky, on Alban Berg, studying a few of Schoenberg's scores, which were available even though one couldn't hear the music. Finally, and that was in 1950, I came to realise that that wasn't satisfactory either: why should I,

[3] Bavarian Radio – Munich
[4] South West Radio – Baden-Baden
[5] West German Radio – Cologne
[6] North German Radio – Hamburg and Hanover

twenty or thirty years after the event, continue in a style that already existed and had already been perfected? And then we had indirect information that totally new ideas were in existence. I heard, although not until later, 1952/53, that electronic music existed, serial music, that there was a person called Cage in America and what he was doing. These were, I would say, snippets of news relayed by someone who had heard it somewhere. Well, that certainly made an impression on me. And at that time I had the first notions of static music, and in fact I was thinking of ceasing to work with melody and harmony, and instead of trying to find a neutralized sound, somewhere between music and noise. Ideas that I later realised in *Atmosphères* I had conceived in almost exactly the same way eleven years previously, but I could not carry them out. The ideas were furthermore restricted because I could not get away from the notion of metrical rhythm; in my first attempts in Budapest, the static planes of sound were still squeezed into a conventional metrical scheme. I still use bars when I compose today, but that is only for practical purposes, so that the works can be conducted. The bars are not bars in the traditional sense, but merely a means of synchronizing the parts. The fact that I did eventually get away from metre and bars, however, was really because of the immediate and very great effect that Boulez and Stockhausen had on me – the music of both of them, and then also my acquaintance with Stockhausen and my first years in Cologne.

H.   So then you carried out these ideas in the orchestral work *Apparitions*?

L.   Yes, that was in '58/59 ...

H.   ... and I should like to suggest that we now hear an excerpt from it.

L.   Then the beginning of the second movement would possibly be a very typical example. It is not as yet an absolutely immobile plane of sound, but rather a plane vibrating within itself, which then dissolves into small figures that appear almost indistinctly, intertwined, and then disappear again.

Musical excerpt: Apparitions, *2nd movement*

L.   I should like to add, apropos of *Apparitions*, that I have used the individual voices in the orchestra, especially the strings, as though they were partials – they are sounds in themselves – as though they were partials of an even more complex sound. Here

90

there is an analogy to the work in the electronic studio. On the other hand, however, my interest in working in the electronic studio was aroused before I knew any electronic music because I already had similar ideas about complex planes of sound. I would put it like this: I sought the opportunity of learning about electronic music, of working with this medium and then returning to instrumental music, because I wanted to apply not the sounds produced from electronic music, but rather the experience gained from working with electronic material. So there is in fact an indirect connection.

H. This path led you subsequently from *Apparitions* to *Atmosphères*. *Atmosphères* was followed by an organ work called *Volumina* in which you further developed the concepts which formed the basis of *Atmosphères*. Is that correct?

L. That is correct. I might say that *Volumina* is a very small tone-colour work, in which the tone-colours are primarily responsible for the organisation of the form. It also has the sustained and static form that was evident in *Atmosphères*, but with the limitations of a single instrument. I experimented in many ways to see what one can produce from this almost defunct instrument and I found that there is still a great deal to be discovered, which was not to be found even in quite advanced works, by, for example, Messiaen. Then there were many possibilities of sliding from one keyboard to the next. This technical feat has an immediate effect on the resulting sound. I should say that that was the last work in which the tone-colour transformations dominated to such an extent. I had come to a point at which I thought: I have worked out definite possibilities for myself now, and if I continue to copy them more and more, I shall have become a plagiarist of myself. And from 1962 I began to ask myself how can I develop my style, and therefore my direction, organically, at the same time shifting the focal point of composition to other spheres?

H. So *Volumina* was, as you have just said, a terminus, and if we now play an example from *Volumina*, may I make a suggestion? I should like to choose a passage where I always have the impression when I am listening to the work that I am hearing not only tone-colours, but also spaces – the title, *Volumina* of course suggests that – and I'd even like to carry the metaphor further and say that it is a passage which conjures up the idea of a thunderstorm of sound. Let us fade in this passage and then return briefly to the matter of the title.

Musical excerpt: Volumina, *1st version, page 12*

H. *Atmosphères* could be described as purely a tone-colour work. *Volumina* for organ is, I think, a work in which colour and space are interrelated. You called one orchestral piece *Lontano*. The title alone suggests spatial aspects. 'Lontano' means 'far' or 'distant': could you give me some sort of a catchphrase for this, which we could then illustrate with a piece of music?

L. For me, spatial associations play a major role in music, but the space is purely imaginary. There are for instance compositions by Cage and Stockhausen – I am thinking particularly of *Gruppen* and *Carré* by Stockhausen – in which actual space plays an essential, even a constructive role. I, on the other hand, had been trying to suggest space, or to generate space by association in my works. And in fact, that isn't anything new in itself. An illusion of space played an important part in romantic music, especially in Mahler. I can think of a passage at the end of the first movement of his Fifth Symphony. There is a trumpet-call, then suddenly silence, then the same trumpet-call can be heard, but transposed to a flute. Well, in terms of actual space, the flautist is sitting just as near or as far from the audience as the trumpeter. And yet, the sound of the flute, with the same musical outline as the trumpet had, seems to us in a purely imaginary fashion to be a trumpet-call from very far away.

H. Please tell me of a passage from *Lontano* in which we can hear particularly clearly the imaginary space that you were trying to convey.

L. In approximately the last third of the work we get, after a static, very soft plane of sound, formed by a major second and a minor third, a gradual passing into dim, deep regions. That in itself creates a strong spatial association. Now, this dark progress is suddenly lightened, as if the music had been illuminated from behind ... I constantly have light-associations which really do play a part in the work ... This progress, once it has begun, goes forwards: the violas, cellos and double-basses carry on the sequence that has started. All the other instruments, and then the cellos as well, take on a new gesture, something suddenly bright, often not perfectly delineated; it gets continually brighter and the music seems to shine, to be radiant. Dynamically, too, this is emphasized by a crescendo, and the pitch by a gradual ascent into higher and higher regions, until a single note, a D sharp, very high up, emerges and stands there, as if this musical light were at first diffuse, but slowly the diffuseness disappears and there is a single directed beam. I am expressing all this by the association of images. At the moment when the high D sharp is there, forming the concentrated 'pencil' of this musical beam, suddenly there yawns an abyss, a huge distancing, a hole piercing through the music. It is a moment that has an irresistible association for me with the wonderful painting by Altdorfer, *The Battle of Alexander* in the Alte Pinakothek in Munich, in which the clouds – these blue clouds – part and behind them there is a beam of golden sunlight shining through. Well, this 'shining through' [in the music] is suddenly interrupted; not entirely, since the high D sharp goes on sounding, but by means of a *subito pianissimo* it seems almost as though a light were turned down, is still there, then goes on fading away into the distance; a light too can die away, a musical light, I mean. And through this suddenly gaping distance and vast expanse can be heard the sound of horns. Well, the horn players are sitting in the normal orchestra pit: the orchestra is not far away; but they sound like something in the distance for various reasons of association. Firstly: after the *fortissimo-tutti* there is suddenly a *pianissimo* and the horns are muted. In addition, the very sound of horns has a 'historical perspective'. Horns coming in like that after a tutti awake in us involuntarily not a direct association perhaps, but an allusion, a reference to certain elements of late romantic music. I am thinking now particularly of Bruckner and Mahler, but also of Wagner. I can think of a passage in Bruckner's Eighth Symphony, in the coda of the slow movement, where with great tranquillity and gentleness the four horns suddenly play a passage that sounds almost like a quotation from Schubert, but seen through Bruckner's eyes. Well, there are many similar – not quotations, but allusions in *Lontano*. I would say that as well as spatial distance, there is also temporal distance; that is to say, we can grasp the work only within our tradition, within a certain musical education. If one were not acquainted with the whole of late Romanticism, the quality of being at a distance, or however I should express it, would not be manifest in this work. For this reason, the piece is double-edged: it is in a sense traditional but not literally as with Stravinsky, it does not treat exact quotations from late romantic music, but certain types of late romantic music are just touched upon. To come back to the spatial effect: the temporal distancing evokes also a spatial distancing. The horns can be heard from a distance and from long ago: almost, as it were, like the post-horn in Mahler's Third Symphony.

Musical excerpt: Lontano, *bars 118–53, score pages 31ff*

H. In speaking about the relationship between your orchestral work *Lontano* and the rest of your work, you used the word 'tone-colour', mentioning *Atmosphères, Volumina* and *Apparitions* in that connection. It would certainly not be wrong to say, therefore, that *Lontano* is also a tone-colour work, although not in the exclusive sense that *Atmosphères* is.

L. In *Atmosphères*, to take an extreme example, the tone-colours were the musical elements pre-eminent in determining the form. In *Lontano* that is not so clearly the case. *Lontano* represents for me a further step in the development of my technique of composition and, indeed, of my concept of composition as it stood in *Atmosphères* and *Volumina*, and this step leads in a quite specific direction. In *Apparitions* and *Atmosphères* I got away from the preoccupation with harmony, or from working with intervals in general. I disrupted the intervals: that is to say, I inserted so many minor seconds that even the minor seconds, or the chromaticism, disappeared in the harmonic sense. It would seem as though I had returned in the more recent works, already from the Requiem and the Cello Concerto onwards and in the choral work *Lux aeterna* and even more clearly in *Lontano*, to an earlier stand-point that I had previously left, namely to working with clearly distinguished intervallic or harmonic configurations. Intervals, definite pitches, really do play an essential role here in the whole basis of the form and also in the image of all the music. The neutralized harmonies – or let us say, the eliminated harmonies, as in *Atmosphères* and *Volumina* – were very rapidly expended. Almost all these works have settled in particular peripheral areas in which one can go no further.

That is, one could go further, but not find anything new. There is a boundary, and then there is the desert; one is standing on this boundary, and if one goes on into the desert, one always finds the same thing: sand. And if you continue going further, you find more of the same thing: sand. If I were to go on composing pieces like *Atmosphères* and *Volumina* now, and working with totally neutralized harmonies, what would I find? Exactly the same thing, that is to say, I would copy myself. Well, I wanted to seek new frontiers. I have to ask myself, why are frontiers so important? Why take an extreme position? I could put it like this: creating something that already exists is not interesting for me. If something new has been tried out and a result has emerged from it, it is not worth making the same experiment again. That would be like a schoolboy repeating the same school chemistry experiment at home – it is nothing but pottering.

As well as searching for new domains, I have a strangely two-edged, or enigmatic relationship to tradition. On the one hand, I deny all musical tradition, and yet subliminally it continues to play a part. For example: *Volumina*, a truly radical work – radical even in the way in which it has been notated in a kind of new, apparently graphic notation, although it has, in fact, nothing to do with graphic notation – *Volumina* sounds different from all earlier organ works. Somewhere, however, under the surface, there remain vestiges of past writing for the organ. In some places you can sense certain baroque figurations, but they are very meandering; Liszt and Reger and the romantic sound of the organ are also there, playing a subliminal role.

H.   Ulrich Dibelius in a book about new music said of you that you were forever striving to solve an equation with at least two unknown factors. What were the unknown factors in *Lontano*?

L.   I could say that one unknown was the way that I was working with intervals and harmonies, that is, with complexes of intervals, in the otherwise neutralized harmonic space. And the other unknown factor would be the polyphony I composed. It is an extensively branching and yet strictly refined polyphony which, however, veers suddenly into something else. In *Atmosphères* it changes into tone-colour, in *Lontano* it has no longer changed exclusively into tone-colour, but into something in between. I don't have a name for it and I don't want to create a term for it. A kind of complex of tone-colour, movement, changing harmonic planes.

Let us talk first about the intervals or complexes of intervals. When in 1962 I came to the frontier district represented by *Volumina* – the total destruction of the intervals – I did not go any further, but began to look for another frontier. I asked myself, how can I work with intervals or with specific fixed pitches without returning to tonal music? That is to say, no chordal development, either in a tonal or an atonal sense. Can one work completely differently from the way in which one has previously worked with intervals or even harmonies that are really worn-out elements? I tried to do so. The first work that is indeed based on a clearly organized structure of intervals is the Requiem. In the Requiem specific connections between the intervals determine the form of the music, without the intervals or complexes of

95

intervals entering into tonal relationships with each other.

I further developed this technique from the Requiem in the a cappella choral work *Lux aeterna*, and one end-product of this was *Lontano*. I believe that *Lontano* is the example that demonstrates most purely the crystallization of corner-stones or pillars that are specific intervals or single notes or harmonies. They provide a kind of contrast to the prevalent neutrality and tone-colour transformation, that is to say, on one level of the work there are tone-colour transformations, but there is another, harmonic level which, I would almost say, is behind it: that is also an aspect of *Lontano*, of being distant. At certain moments in the work there are single pitches or groups of intervals. To give you one example: at the very beginning I proceed from a certain note – an A flat. This A flat then plays a role in the work as a whole. If you then look for similar corner-stones later on, you find that all twelve notes emerge as pillars. That has nothing to do with twelve-note music – there is no note-row. It is merely a question of fitting all the twelve notes somewhere into the work: each of them as an element as yet unused. There are, of course, connections with dodecaphony, but it isn't dodecaphony in the usual sense. So, to return to the beginning of the work: we hear a single pitch that is clearly there, but gradually it becomes rather cloudy, rather hazy, because 'parasitic' pitches are joined to it: as well as A flat, we get G, then B flat, A and so on – all different pitches. And because of the fact that more and more adjacent pitches are played and because, besides that, the ensemble of strings is divided into many single instruments, the result is small deviations in intonation. For example, it is a known fact that a violinist going from C to C sharp and then to D, involuntarily makes the C sharp higher. The small deviations that result in this involuntary manner are here a constructive element in the composition. I haven't used any quarter-tones; of course, there may be some, but it was of no importance to me exactly how much the pitches deviate. So if I say the work is notated in equal temperament, but doesn't sound like it, I have indicated a general aspect of my musical conception, namely the relationship to the finished artefact. The music has something artificial about it: it is an illusion. There are many elements in it that don't manifest themselves, but remain subliminal. Thus the opening note of the work appears to be continuous, but this is not really the case, for the instruments change. The tone-colour of the work varies – that is the aspect of tone-colour transformation and it is gradually dissolved, almost as if I were throwing a salt crystal into water.

Musical excerpt: Lontano, *bars 1–44, score page 7ff*

H.   Would you now like to describe the subsequent progress of the work to me?
L.   In its intervals or harmonies, the work has the following structure: there are certain places in which a pitch or an interval or even several intervals – let us use the old-fashioned term 'chords' – are clearly to be heard. Then in the middle of a chord the 'parasitic' notes gradually sound; they are not ornamental in the sense of the passing notes or auxiliary notes of tonal music, but they do contain a slight allusion to them. The whole tradition of tonal music is present, but always hidden. Now this intervallic or harmonic plane gradually clouds over, and this cloudiness expands more and more, until finally the originally pellucid, clear harmonic structure dissolves into an opaque plane. In the middle of this opaque or neutral plane we then get signs of a new constellation of pitches which by degrees becomes more and more dominant. At first, the new constellation is barely audible. Gradually, however, the different parts gather together into the individual intervals which are later revealed in a bright light. That is to say, there is a harmonic transformation in a similar way to the tone-colour transformation in my earlier works. So I am of the opinion that this is not a return to traditional intervallic and harmonic music, but rather that harmony and intervals are treated as though they were tone-colours.
H.   Could we listen to an example of one of these harmonic transformations?

Musical excerpt: Lontano, *bars 56–113, score page 17ff*

H.   Would you like to describe to me in detail how this harmonic transformation is achieved?
L.   The passage corresponds roughly to the middle of the piece, but it represents the harmonic technique of the whole work. At the beginning, I took a single note then gradually dissolved it. Something similar happens here, but instead of using a single note as the point of departure, it is now an interval. This interval is a tritone: E to B flat, to be precise, over several octaves. I must add that in general in this work I use a multiple octave doubling of the instruments that produces a particularly soft sound. This is essential for the way in which the harmony is dissolved. I am not concerned with a soft sound as in the large orchestras of romantic

music; rather, my whole conception of the work is as follows: I dissolve these 'harmonic crystals' and let new harmonies become cystallized – I am now speaking figuratively of fluid crystals: formations that have a crystalline structure, but which nevertheless dissolve; and so, in order to create this soft process of dissolution, I have a predilection for using multiple octave doubling or an organ-like 'registration' of the orchestra.

In the last example, we heard as the point of departure a clear constellation of pitches, the tritone E to B flat. The note E as well as the note B flat are now blurred by the neighbouring notes which gradually emerge. Then the multiplying of the octaves increases constantly so that the compass of the music expands, yet you don't perceive this as something suddenly intruding – rather as a gradual process. Dissolution, expansion, broadening of the compass, as though the music were increasing in circumference – now I am practically returning to my own quotation about *Atmosphères*: the whole is dissolved in an atmospheric plane of sound. But within this plane of sound we have again, almost hidden, little references to definite intervals, and these intervals are exposed melodically as well as simultaneously, therefore, harmonically. Some of the more penetrative instruments – an oboe, for example, or the English horn, or suddenly a solo violin – are involuntarily brought into prominence. There is a passage in approximately the middle of this whole development when the four horns, then three trumpets and three trombones enter with a little melodic flourish that we hear and yet don't hear: major second and minor third underneath – we just hear a suggestion of them through the web of sound. Much later in the work one will be able to hear the major second and the minor third very clearly, but now, in this development, they remain hidden under the surface or 'behind the music'. So here I return to the essence of *Lontano*, of 'distance'. Behind the music there is other music, and behind that more still – a kind of infinite perspective, as if one saw oneself in two mirrors, with the never-ending reflection that this produces.

H. If I understand you aright, the mirrors move, allowing some things that have been in the background to come forward, and others that have been in the foreground to retreat into the background again, so that there is a kind of fluctuation.

L. Yes, yes, that is absolutely right, and that was my original idea. *Atmosphères* was to a large extent grey: it was colourful in the sense of tone-colour, but harmonically grey; in *Lontano*, on the other hand, both tone-colour and harmony are colourful.

H. When I compare the orchestral work *Lontano* with *Atmosphères*, I have the impression that in *Lontano* the individual instrumental parts bear a far greater responsibility than in *Atmosphères*. Is this impression correct and is the second unknown factor connected with it, namely your work with polyphonic modes of composition?

L. Yes, definitely. In *Atmosphères* the individual instrumentalists sustain long notes for the most part, and are responsible for the dynamic alteration of these notes, but they do not have any function as soloists. *Lontano* is a work for a big orchestra, but one could say that it is for an orchestra composed of nothing but soloists. It is not a question of functioning as soloists in the sense of being virtuosi, but rather that each musician in this divided orchestra has a particular responsibility for the separate, expressive formation of his particular part. That is why I dedicated the work to the Südwestfunk Symphony Orchestra: the musicians in the orchestra are the true soloists of the work.

In several of my more recent works from the Requiem onwards, that is from the year 1963, I have a tendency to use the following device in my compositions: I propose something, expound something, begin something, and yet before it really exists, I take it back. Now, how does that happen, in a purely technical sense? In the following way: I set out as though a 'theme' or a 'great expansive melody' were now about to occur, and yet thinking in terms of themes is entirely alien to this music. There is only the rudimentary stage, suggesting that a theme is about to appear. So everything, before being quite expressed, is immediately withdrawn again. This brings me to the question of polyphony itself. Technically, *Lontano* is a completely and strictly structured polyphonic work: that is to say, there is a definite part-writing, there are vertical relationships between the parts and the individual instrumentalists play their parts as autonomous units. Through the complex overlapping and interweaving of the parts, however, the listener loses sight of them, although perhaps not entirely; that is to say, the traces of this polyphony remain audible. The polyphony in itself is not audible; I mean, polyphony like that of the Dutch school, or of Palestrina's or Bach's music is not to be found here. I would say that the polyphony is dissolved – like the harmony and the tone-colour – to such an extent that it does not manifest itself, and yet it is there, just beneath the threshold.

H. I would suggest that we now listen to an example of this contrapuntal allusion, if I may call it that, from *Lontano* – perhaps the beginning.

L. Yes. The passage we heard before can now be heard completely differently if, instead of concentrating on how the orginal note, A flat, expands into a harmonic complex, we concentrate on what is happening in the individual parts. If we listen very carefully, we shall notice that the instruments entering one after another – flutes, clarinets, then strings, finally an oboe and then strings again and more and more instruments – are all playing the same melody but not at the same time. As far as the pitch is concerned, there is here a rigorously executed canon structure.

Musical excerpt: Lontano, *bars 1–44, page 7ff*

H. We spoke of polyphonic allusion, but you expressed it a little differently: 'Polyphony is written, but harmony is heard.' Why do you compose polyphony that cannot be heard?

L. That's a very valid question, and I could argue with myself about it. Why do I write such definite, detailed orchestral parts?

H. Yes, and one can extend the question even further. In *Atmosphères* where there are actually only planes of sound, the individual parts are written out in the minutest detail, without in fact being audible as individual parts in this detailed way.

L. Yes, it is apparently a contradiction. For me, too, it would be much simpler and, I might almost say, a more economical way of composing if I used a system of 'generalized' notation such as that used by Penderecki. When a cluster is played by one group of instruments, let us say a high cluster in the violins, a small indication shows which instrument plays what note; this cluster is notated in a generalized manner and if there are then changes of pitch, the pattern of notation is changed, is shifted, that is, everyone playing *glissando*, etc. It is a very economical, practical and sufficient notation for the type of music that Penderecki composes. But for the kind of music that I compose, it is not adequate, for the following reason: I want to be able to steer the course of each separate part myself . . .

H. So you want to direct the internal fluctuation within a plane in an entirely conscious way . . .

L. . . . to steer and direct it entirely consciously. And that was my intention with the hidden polyphony as well. Within these planes there is a polyphony that has been developed in the

100

composition and which appears in the score, but is not immediately audible; we hear not the polyphony itself, but its result. If I were to notate that in an undifferentiated way, the result would not be the same. As an example I should like to make this comparison: only a very small part of an iceberg is visible, the largest part being hidden under the water. But what the iceberg looks like, how it moves, how it is affected by various currents in the ocean, all these things are determined not only by the visible, but also by the invisible part. That is why I call my method of composing and notating uneconomical, indeed somewhat prodigal. I specify many details that are not in themselves audible. But the fact that I have specified these details is essential for the general result – at least, that is what I hope. I think of a large architectural edifice in which many details are not visible. For the general result, for the formal quality of the structure as a whole, they nevertheless play an important role. Music is for me in the first instance something intuitive. Then, however, I begin to work conceptually, making concrete the original purely acoustic or musical vision. In finding a conceptual development that matches the musical vision, during which I prescribe rules for myself as to composition or form, something concrete emerges from the general vision, and that is the score. At the performance, however, there is a shift back to the original, general vision. So I do in the end hear the sound that I had had in my mind. In between the two, a rational product, so to say, has been manufactured. It is precisely this tension between the rational, constructed element on the one hand, the visionary on the other, that plays such an important role in composing for me.

H. You wrote in *Melos* in 1967: 'The involuntary transposing of optical and tactile sensations into acoustic equivalents occurs very often with me. I almost always associate sounds with colour, form and consistency, just as, on the other hand, for every acoustic sensation I find form, colour and a material quality.' This interrelationship of synaesthetic moments, this effect of crossing from one sense-impression to another sensual area, accordingly plays an important part in your work of composition, or perhaps rather in your musical intuition?

L. Yes, certainly, but here I must both complete the picture and limit it a little. Pronouncements like this, the way that I speak about music, could be misunderstood as being programmatic. So that I would then be composing a kind of programme music. But it is certainly not that. I could put it in this way: the relationships between different sense-impressions, tactile, olfactory, visual, acoustic, certainly play a major part. Whenever I listen to music, I see colours and shapes. But that does not signify that it is literary or illustrative music in the sense of programme music. If I say, for example, that *Lontano* is a work in which colours and space are very significant, these colours and this space exist only in the music. *Lontano*, distance, remoteness, as an aura of feeling that surrounds this music, is to be understood as a purely musical category. It has nothing to do with programme music as in Liszt, Berlioz or Strauss, for example. If I were to mention Debussy and Mahler, two composers whom I especially love, I would say that their music brings in its wake, as a comet in its train, a whole wide area of associations from every level of human experience. In this way, music or the artificial product, 'a work of art', is truly bound for me with every stratum of imagination and of actual life. But everything is transposed into music! So I would say: Programme music without a programme, music that is developed extensively in its associations, yet pure music. Everything that is direct and unambiguous is alien to me. I love allusions, equivocal utterances, things that have many interpretations, uncertainties, background meanings. And the various figurative associations in my music are also ambiguous, as I see them, think them or feel them while I imagine music.

II[7]

H. Mr Ligeti, the word 'string quartet' in itself evokes a whole chain of associations. It might begin, for example, with the famous simile by Goethe, in which the string quartet is likened to a discussion between four intelligent people. Yet string quartets also make one think at the same time of a number of works which represent particular peaks in the whole repertory of chamber-music. Perhaps the word is even connected with the association of the noblest, purest form of chamber-music. And finally, string quartets call to mind the domestic, idyllic musical scene. Mr Ligeti, how does it feel to compose a string quartet in 1968?
L. Well, I could say this: the genre, string quartet, imposes a commitment because of the great tradition with which it is

[7] Interview between György Ligeti and Josef Häusler, recorded by the Südwestfunk, Baden-Baden, on 14 December 1969, shortly before the première of the Second String Quartet

burdened. After Beethoven's last quartets, or Bartók's fourth and fifth quartets, or the *Lyric Suite*, or after Schoenberg, one hardly dares to write another quartet. Yet, despite this burden of tradition I still wanted to compose such a work; in fact, it is my second, and I could enumerate various aspects that induced me to compose this new string quartet. But I must say at once, it is not a string quartet in the sense of 'Hausmusik'. The concept of 'domestic music' is in any case fairly alien to me.

H. You said just now that the tradition of the late Beethoven quartets, the quartets by Bartók, the *Lyric Suite*, impose such a heavy commitment that one hardly dares to write another string quartet. Despite this, you dared. How do you see the position of your String Quartet in the light of this tradition?

L. Here we come to a question that is important not only in connection with my String Quartet, but with all my works in recent years. I have a strangely ambivalent attitude towards tradition. On the one hand I create music that is not traditional, that is – at least I hope so – something new or personal. Fine, everybody hopes that, but whether or not one succeeds is a different matter. I try to create something new, because composing once again something that has already been composed is totally uninteresting. That applies just as much to my own works. I could no longer today write something of the same kind as I did a few years ago – the orchestral works *Apparitions* and *Atmosphères*. I want to go further and further in my own way of composition. That does not mean that I want to change my style, but that within a carefully determined stylistic possibility or stylistic path I try to go further and further. And when I say 'go further' I don't now mean development, but simply different new aspects, or new solutions to problems of composition. There are, of course, some of my works that are related to earlier pieces: for example, my Cello Concerto. Its first movement is closely connected to the choral work *Lux aeterna* or to the orchestral work *Atmosphères*. *Lontano*, too, is related to these two works, namely in its stationary form. But within this relationship there were always new aspects for me in each new composition. *Lontano* and *Atmosphères*, for example – two works in the stationary form where only very gradually does any change creep in and every rhythmical element is concealed – were nevertheless two totally different solutions to the same formal idea. *Atmosphères* with the technique of largely chromatically constructed, very complex sounds – the term 'sound' is possibly not at all appropriate for this (I have used the word 'sonority', meaning neither noise, nor sound, but something in between the two) and *Lontano*, very similar in form, but completely different in its musical substance: for here I work with harmonies, with definite transformations of harmonies, which wasn't the case in *Atmosphères*.

H. Now, you said before that you had a double-edged attitude to tradition. How is that reflected in your Second String Quartet?

L. In almost all my works composed in the last three or four years there is some kind of allusion to traditional style; not direct quotations, but really hints, allusions. In the orchestral work *Lontano* there were repeated allusions to the whole aura of late romantic music, especially to Mahler, but also to Wagner and Bruckner. Similarly, in my String Quartet there are allusions to earlier string quartets. These allusions may be relatively concrete, as for example in the last movement (the work has five movements of very varied character). There we have more or less clear allusions to Bartók's string quartet style, just as in the *Largo desolato* of Berg's *Lyric Suite* there is a quite open allusion to *Tristan*, in fact *Tristan* is literally quoted. But in fact this quotation is not the essential thing, it is rather the whole line-drawing which represents a kind of transfigured Wagner . . . And my allusions to Bartók are a bit like that. I don't want to deny that I was greatly influenced by Bartók, particularly in my early days, and this String Quartet contains a quite intentional little homage to Bartók. His music is not quoted, but its aura is present within a context that is quite different. Bartók still composed in a truly thematic and motivic manner, almost in the Beethoven sense, even though his technique was no longer tonal. But this thematic-motivic technique is not to be found in my String Quartet at all. Instead, in my String Quartet, I remain true to my 'plane of sound' technique or to the micropolyphonic method of composition; by which I mean, there are very finely interwoven and complex nets, although they cannot be nearly as complex in a quartet as in a work for full orchestra. In works for a large ensemble, such as *Atmosphères* or *Lontano* or the Requiem, the net is much more complex, but the part-writing is much simpler. In the String Quartet, however, the types of motion within the nets are much more complex. I think I could say that the Quartet is the most difficult work that I have composed to date.

May I now return to the previous question: the responsibilities imposed by the string quartet as a genre? In the first place, one is bound to attain a quite specific standard. After Beethoven, Schoenberg, Bartók, Webern – one could name others as well: Schubert or Brahms...

H. ... Haydn, Mozart ...

L. ... it's odd that I haven't mentioned the string quartets by Haydn and Mozart, although it is precisely them that I love more than ... well, I also love Beethoven, I love all good music ... it's difficult to say.

H. So the string quartet entails responsibilities. You wanted to enumerate a few points about that.

L. Well, one is obliged to attain a certain standard in composition. Ever since Beethoven the composition of a string quartet has become a kind of test for every composer: how great is one's potential in that genre? I am now not referring to technical capabilities in composition, but rather to the purely spiritual aspect. For a long time I had been lured by the idea of composing a string quartet for this very reason: I wanted to put my own standard to the test. I do not want to appear to measure myself against these distinguished traditional models, but I would nevertheless like to say that string quartets like Berg's *Lyric Suite*, Bartók's Fourth and Fifth String Quartets and – not in a formal sense but in so far as their structural standard is concerned – also Webern's quartets, and especially the Bagatelles, these have been touchstones for me. Yes, and then Debussy's String Quartet, music which hasn't a broken-up texture as in Beethoven or Berg; yet, as far as the standard of composition is concerned, the Debussy Quartet is also an unattainable example of unbelievable richness. That is one point. Now I come to the second. I have already anticipated it a little – my ambivalent attitude to tradition: denying tradition by creating something new, and yet at the same time allowing tradition to shine through indirectly through allusions: that is essential for me. In *Atmosphères* for example it was Debussy to a large extent, in *Lontano* Debussy too, but perhaps more the late romantics who shone through. Then there were other works, for example *Aventures* and *Nouvelles Aventures* in which traditional opera, Rossini and Verdi, all of it was there somewhere, but very indirectly. Or in the organ work *Volumina* the great works by Bach like the Passacaglia were present, but very, very hidden. I don't know how one can explain that psychologically. Perhaps I somewhere harbour the need, when I cut myself off from tradition so radically, to maintain secretly an umbilical cord, like an astronaut who is bound by a cord to the satellite, although he moves about freely in space. Perhaps for that reason there are the allusions to Bartók, to the *Lyric Suite*, also to late Beethoven or for example to the C-major Quartet by Mozart, the 'Dissonance quartet'. But I feel rather ashamed of myself: I have been speaking now only about very great music. But at any rate, these were the examples that sprang to mind.

H.   Mr Ligeti, basically we live in an age of one-movement forms. You yourself have composed a whole series of one-movement compositions.

L.   Yes, most of my works have only one movement.

H.   What caused you in this instance to return to a work with several movements? Another allusion to tradition?

L.   No; the fact that this Quartet has several movements has nothing to do with earlier quartets having had several movements. I could just as easily have composed a one-movement quartet; there are many examples in the more recent repertoire. The fact that I composed several movements in this work is an immediate result of its characteristics of motion, and in saying this we arrive at another topic. When we were testing the microphone earlier you mentioned that this Quartet differs considerably from my previous works and that is true. I believe that here, although I remain faithful to the technique I have used hitherto, I nevertheless found certain new solutions to questions that concern the whole concept of form.

H.   Would you like to describe this concept of form to me in a little more detail?

L.   My earlier works, that is from the second half of the 1950s onwards, were characterized by two opposing types of form or motion, or let us say, musical types. On the one hand, there were the completely static forms. An example of this is *Atmosphères*, where the musical form is very long drawn-out and extremely delicate internal changes determine the formal structure; that is to say, the music does not develop but becomes 'stationary'. Then there is the type which contrasts with that: music that is totally broken up and splintered. Examples of this are the *Dies irae* from the Requiem or the two pieces *Aventures* and *Nouvelles Aventures*. Here there is no development either, these are 'stationary' as well, but each 'state' is very short-lived. In many of my works you find the repeated instruction: *Stop suddenly, as though broken off.* Actually, the splintered type and the stationary one are two versions of the same musical type, two extremes. And if I

106

say now that I have been trying in the past few years to unite these two extremes, I don't mean this in the sense of a synthesis. I would say rather that from these two previous types of motion I have gradually come to other types that are neither totally static, nor abruptly changing. But there had already been the seeds of these types of motion in earlier works: in *Apparitions*, for example, in which immobility is followed by very quickly occurring changes. I would venture to say that *Apparitions* is the first work in the typical Ligeti style. Many people believe that essential to this is the tone-colour technique of composition, but I think that for me the technique of a very complex polyphonic net-formation is of primary importance. I have always used this kind of polyphony – in the String Quartet as well, for you find there the typical Ligeti micropolyphony, that is, the very dense polyphonic net-formations. They have, however, become more transparent. I had done that previously in earlier works, and it can be seen clearly in the Cello Concerto. In the second movement of the Cello Concerto there is a gradual loosening of this complex net-formation: it is neither a completely stationary, nor a totally disrupted form. I think that the consequences of this second movement of the Cello Concerto led me to new works with several movements, for example the String Quartet and on the other hand the *Ten Pieces for Wind Quintet*, very short pieces, differing widely from each other in their type of motion. I wanted to realize one and the same thought, one and the same musical concept in the five movements of the String Quartet and so to relate them to one another. The same musical idea is carried out in five totally different ways, and so I arrive at an articulation of the overall form. In the first movement, the structure is largely broken up, as in the Requiem or in *Aventures*: one could almost describe it as an instrumental variant of these works. In the second movement everything is reduced to very slow motion. It is no longer completely static, as in my earlier compositions; there are also different turning-points and sudden changes, but in relation to the first movement, it seems as though the music were now coming from a distance. The third movement is a pizzicato piece. This is possibly the clearest allusion to Bartók's Fourth Quartet with its pizzicato movement. But apart from the piz-zicato, there are no further connections with Bartók. The net-formations which were very soft until this point, now become hard and mechanical; the movement is like a machine that breaks down. I have done that before in various works – in *Continuum* for harpsichord and in *Ramifications*.

H. What strikes me particularly in the third movement is the multilayered progress of time.

L. After *Atmosphères* and *Volumina* when I had composed 'soft' music, I felt an ever-increasing inclination towards definitely 'hard', mechanical processes. And important in this was the fact that I reacted against the over-sensitization of rhythm in the serial music of the middle 1950s. I wanted to get rid of rhythm as a concept altogether. In works like *Apparitions* and *Atmosphères*, there are of course rhythmical processes in the individual parts, but they are generally neutralized; the music appears to be continually flowing, with no rhythmical fluctuation any longer, and as a subsequent, new reaction against this abolition of rhythmical figures, I later thought of working with rhythm again – not rhythm in its former sense, but a kind of exaggerated rhythm, with completely automated rhythmical processes. In 1962, immediately after *Atmosphères* and *Volumina*, I composed a work for 100 metronomes; well, that was a kind of persiflage, an automatic concerto for 100 pieces of apparatus, a persiflage on 'happenings', but also on official concerts. Yet if you listen now to the work for metronomes, after hearing the pizzicato movement from the String Quartet or the work for harpsichord, *Continuum*, you realise that the piece for metronomes was a preparatory stage for this pizzicato-movement. My work for string orchestra *Ramifications* also has many mechanical procedures like that. Now a mechanical procedure in itself is quite without interest. But what attracts me is the idea of superimposing several levels, several different time-grids moving at different speeds, and so very subtly achieving rhythmical deviations. That is what I meant when I said the machine breaks down. I did not mean it in a programmatic sense; my third movement is not 'machine-music', but there are certain allusions to the automation in which we live. I should like to say something more about that: it was nothing new to have different tempi running together. That is very characteristic of Ives's music when he puts different layers on top of one another: not only rhythmical layers, but also layers of tempi, or several marches together, as in *Decoration Day* or in *The Fourth of July* or in the middle movement of *Three Places in New England*. That is wonderful, and I must admit that I love Ives very much, particularly this clashing of different marches. In Mahler's Third Symphony, at the end of the development of the first movement when various marches are interrupting each other, as it were – there we have the same idea.

H. You have spoken now at some length about the third movement. But I should still like to hear you say something about the remaining two movements. How would you characterize the fourth movement?

L. I should like briefly to recapitulate the types of motion: in the first movement, abrupt, very sharp switches of fast and slow, in the second movement the same material slowly, in the third movement the same material broken up, as it were, into a kind of grill or grid system. The fourth movement is a very brutal movement, *presto* and *minaccioso*, that is to say, very fast and very threatening. Everything that happened before is now crammed together. In astronomy there are dwarf stars: the same mass that is contained in our sun is compressed into a millionth part of the volume and has an incredible density, but it is still the same mass. And the fifth movement – in great contrast to the compressed fourth – spreads itself out just, just . . . like a cloud. The last movement has the most connections with my earlier music; I am thinking especially of *Atmosphères*, of something very soft, therefore, but in the String Quartet the process is not so static. There are quite definite movements and directions in it; it is very quiet and fades away into nothingness, in a kind of mist. In each movement the same basic configurations return, in fact, but their colouring is different, or the viewpoint is different, so that what is actually the overall musical form only really emerges when one listens to all five movements in context. In order to facilitate listening to the whole work, I should like to mention one detail: at the end of the first movement, there is one particular type of motion: until then there was a very fast motion, a kind of very energetic, compressed process, and that gradually comes to a standstill; it is like a kind of braking, or like an air-balloon that has been pricked with a needle and that gradually collapses. These directions of motion are essential to my musical ideas. I mean all that in a metaphorical way: I think only in music and not in descriptions like that. But the collapse at the end of the first movement returns as a variant at the end of the second movement. It is like a rhyme between two lines of a poem. At the end of the first movement the motion of the music gradually subsides and the sounds change into harmonics. The same thing happens in the second movement in a varied form. Again in the third movement: the pizzicato recedes, and even the fifth movement fades away. Only the fourth movement does not follow this gradually subsiding form, simply because it is so condensed. It ends very abruptly. Everything that has happened before is completely cut in pieces. It is, if you like, a little allusion to Stravinsky's *Sacre*.

(1968/69)   *Translation from German by Sarah E. Soulsby*

3

Samuel: Now that *Le Grand Macabre*, your first opera, has been launched on an international career, now that it is about to enter the repertory of the Palais Garnier, can you retrace your itinerary in the operatic field?

Ligeti: Opera is a very traditional genre. The great tradition goes from Monteverdi through Mozart, Verdi and Wagner to end up with Berg. Personally, of course, I have always been very interested in music theatre but I also like traditional opera. As regards my own activity as a composer, I created a few 'happenings' in the '60s – after all, it was very much the thing to do. Then I wrote *Aventures* and *Nouvelles Aventures*, pieces which can either be performed on the concert platform or produced on the stage (although I prefer the former) – experimental pieces the text of which is semantically without meaning. That was the period when Mauricio Kagel was showing the way towards a new music theatre and I had the feeling that it was impossible to compose a real opera for a big theatre and a big stage. Kagel's *Staatstheater*, first performed in Hamburg in 1971, was a crucial point in this development: it's the masterpiece of 'musical anti-theatre'; and it was *Staatstheater* which gave me the idea of writing an 'anti-anti-opera'. Since 'anti-opera' in the style of *Staatstheater* or *Aventures* was already outmoded, my 'anti-opera' therefore became an 'anti-anti-opera', and since two successive 'antis' cancel each other out, it ended up as 'opera'!

Although *Le Grand Macabre* is more traditional than *Aventures* and *Nouvelles Aventures*, I think it is still part of the continuity of experimental music, but at the same time it is linked to classical opera, especially Monteverdi and Mozart and to some extent Verdi – that is to say that it stands on the opposite side of the line Wagner-Strauss-Berg. I may add that it isn't a literary opera, and yet it's closely related to the theatrical conceptions of Jarry, Artaud and Ionesco. In addition, *Le Grand Macabre* is

111

related to cinema – for instance, the Charlie Chaplin figure – to film cartoons and comic strips. Let's say that music-theatre was an abstract genre and that I wanted to return to a certain narrative style.

S. Can we go back over the succession of influences in order to establish the links that connect *Le Grand Macabre* to the operatic tradition? What are the crowning moments in that tradition that have impressed themselves on you?

L. It was in Cluj, the capital of Transylvania, where I lived from my sixth to my twentieth year, that I had my first contact with opera. There were two Operas in Cluj, a Romanian opera house and a Hungarian operetta theatre – for three languages, Romanian, Hungarian and German, were spoken in Transylvania. From the age of seven I used to be taken to the opera to hear such works as *La Traviata*, *Il Trovatore* and *Rigoletto*, but the first opera I saw was *Boris Godunov*. This performance of *Boris* is one of my great childhood memories, but of course I was mainly impressed by the coronation scene and the great peal of the bells. I was also seven years old when we first started hearing early recordings of operas at home, though in that period of 78s it was a matter of extracts lasting a few minutes: Verdi, Mozart, Wagner. As it happened, at the Cluj Opera they didn't play Mozart and Wagner: people preferred Verdi and Bizet. Personally, I was very fond of *Carmen*, but certainly not *Les Pêcheurs de Perles*.

Then I became a composer and opera wasn't at the centre of my preoccupations. However, I had discovered the operas of Mozart, though Wagner remained a closed book to me. And it was again Mozart that I heard as a student in Budapest, thanks to Klemperer who was then the musical director of the Opera: *Le Nozze di Figaro*, *Così fan tutte* and above all *Don Giovanni*, which was for me the ideal opera. Much later I discovered Monteverdi. And I can say today that for me the four essential operas are *L'Incoronazione di Poppea*, *Don Giovanni*, *Figaro* and *Falstaff*. I might add a fifth: *Otello*; and perhaps a sixth: *Carmen*.

S. For years people have been talking of the difficulties encountered by the composers of this century, and in particular the most ambitious of them, in trying to establish a contemporary operatic idiom. And yet we have had *Pelléas*, *Wozzeck*, *Lulu* and Schoenberg's operas.

L. Some years ago, Boulez declared that opera-houses should be blown up, that opera was dead. I agreed with him, and I still

112

do. As regards Alban Berg, I must say straight out, even if my judgement is considered blasphemous, that although I greatly admire and respect Berg's music, *Wozzeck* and *Lulu* are not my taste, because in the final analysis they are too literary. For me, the characters in opera live both in the libretto and the music, thanks to a close combination of the two elements. Monteverdi, Mozart and Verdi created real characters. Don Giovanni and Leporello are truly living characters; they already exist in Da Ponte's libretto, but the characterization of their inner lives comes primarily from Mozart's music. Is it unjust of me to aver that in the twentieth century no one has brought off the synthesis of music and text as Mozart and Verdi did? I like *Wozzeck* very much, more than *Lulu*; I recognize that it's a fantastic score: but I don't feel the motivation of this music. No, really, twentieth-century opera, of which Berg is the outstanding representative, doesn't interest me. I prefer anti-opera, the challenge of Kagel, the experiments of Harry Partch, and also really popular works.

S.   Musical comedies?

L.   Yes, musical comedies. I'm thinking of *Porgy and Bess*, a work that is very naïve but very alive, like Verdi's operas. And I've forgotten Puccini! I don't like his music – too kitsch for me – but an opera like *La Bohème* is based on real feelings, real situations, real characters.

S.   And what about Janáček's characters?

L.   I admire Janáček's operas – not *Jenufa*, which is too folksy, but *The Makropoulos Affair*, which is living theatre, though not on the level of Mozart and Verdi. And *The House of the Dead*, a marvellous score, though the end result is static.

S.   Does opera as a musical form no longer suit the contemporary composer?

L.   Yes, I think opera is a bit outmoded; it's a museum where the public goes to hear Wagner and Verdi. *Le Grand Macabre* certainly has its outmoded aspects. In fact I may say that in the hands of certain producers it may seem like a traditional opera. This is not what i want. I prefer productions of *Le Grand Macabre* to be inspired by strip-cartoons, pop art, Charlie Chaplin, the Marx brothers, in a spirit of farce, but a sort of demoniac farce – I might cite as an example the Bologna production, with designs and costumes by Topor. This is not a criticism of the other productions – there have been five up to now – but the Bologna one really caught the spirit of the work; it was a demoniacal romp, a great extravaganza.

S.   The productions of *Le Grand Macabre* are the end product of a long development. Can you remember the origins of *Le Grand Macabre*, the stages of its conception and composition?

L.   It's a long story. In 1965, Göran Gentele, who was then the director of the Stockholm Opera (later he became director of the Metropolitan Opera), asked me to write an opera and my first idea was to continue along the lines of *Aventures*, to compose a non-narrative work. But how to transpose *Aventures* and *Nouvelles Aventures* into a work for a big theatre? It seemed an insurmountable stylistic problem. Then I thought of an opera called *Kilwiria*, from the name of an imaginary country with which I had toyed during my childhood. It would be a crazy, demoniacal, cruel but also humorous piece, a non-narrative piece modelled on *Aventures*.

S.   But nothing was composed...

L.   No, I turned the project over in my mind for two years; I thought up various situations; then I abandoned it. Since I envisaged a large-scale piece, the absence of narration posed a problem; I had to find a dramatic thread. It was then, around 1968, that I became tempted by the Greek myths which offered the advantage of being at once totally familiar and sending me back to other musical works: Monteverdi, Gluck, Stravinsky. I chose Oedipus and I wrote a scenario, a sort of synopsis, as well as a certain number of musical sketches for a narrative opera the text of which, however, as with *Aventures*, was not semantically significant. I devoted several years to this project.

S.   But without result...

L.   Without result. In 1972, Gentele died in a motor-car accident and the shock of his death interrupted my work. Then I realised that I was heading towards a dead end. As I said before, I had just been impressed by Kagel's *Staatstheater* and the anti-opera on which I was working was undermined by this new departure. It became clear to me that I must opt for an opera with a text, while circumventing the norms of traditional opera.

S.   And suddenly you hit upon the work of Ghelderode.

L.   Well, the team responsible for putting on the work I was to write for Stockholm had in fact already been formed. Michael Meschke, the director of the Puppet Theatre, had been chosen as producer, Aliute Meczies was responsible for the designs and costumes and Elgar Howarth was to be the conductor. One day Meschke, Meczies and I foregathered in Berlin, together with the Swedish musicologist Nordwall, in search of a suitable text. I was looking for something cruel and frightening; I was thinking of the *Dies irae* from the Requiem, of images based on the pictures of Brueghel and Bosch, the works of Jarry, Kafka, Boris Vian.

S. That's the family all right ...

L. Yes, it's my family, to which I might also add a few Hungarian writers, in particular the great contemporary poet Sándor Weöres. Then, one day, *La Balade du Grand Macabre* came to my attention and it was exactly what I was looking for. At last I had found a play about the end of the world, a bizarre, demoniacal, cruel and also very comic piece, to which I wanted to give an additional dimension, that of ambiguity. Thus, with the character of Nekrozotar, whom I transform into Nekrotzar, the tsar of the dead, one never knows whether he really represents death or whether he is simply a charlatan.

So *Le Grand Macabre* is an opera about death conceived as a farce. And indeed this is precisely what Ghelderode himself had in mind. But in Ghelderode's play Nekrozotar is really a charlatan, whereas in my opera I leave an element of doubt, which is feasible thanks to music.

S. What were the different stages between Ghelderode's text and the final libretto?

L. The first stage revolved round the choice of the language to be used for the final libretto. My native tongue is Hungarian, but the rhythms of the Hungarian language are so idiosyncratic that translation is impossible – it's the same problem with Janáček's Czech. For me, Italian and English are the two ideal languages for opera – especially English, the rhythms of which are very flexible – but I am more familiar with German. The première was to take place in Sweden and *Le Grand Macabre* thus had to be sung in Swedish, and it struck me that, without being exactly superimposable, the rhythms of German and the rhythms of Swedish were fairly close. Since its completion the opera has been translated into three languages: Italian, French and English. The Italian and the French presented a number of rhythmic problems and I had to make some musical modifications, particularly in the distribution of the rhythms.

At the outset, it was Meschke who, thanks to his perfect command of both German and Swedish, and also of French, produced a German prose version on the basis of Ghelderode's original – a version that I might describe as 'Jarryfied', having myself suggested to Meschke that he should model himself on the very terse, very direct speech of *Ubu Roi*. Ghelderode's Rabelaisian language, which is perfect for the spoken theatre, is too rich and flowery to be set to music; moreover, the original text was too long for an opera libretto, so Meschke reduced the original three acts to two acts each comprising two scenes.

S. Did you intervene in the course of Meschke's work?

L. I followed Meschke's libretto except for the ending. I suggested that the identity of Nekrotzar should remain in doubt, and he accepted my suggestion. Later I transformed Meschke's prose libretto into rhyming verse while at the same time composing the score. Thus a musical idea could introduce words possessing a particular rhythmic structure; it was a method that I had already applied in the case of *Aventures* and *Nouvelles Aventures*. I must confess that I had to use dictionaries of synonyms and rhymes because my German has its weaknesses. My friends at Schott's made a few corrections and then said: 'It isn't very good German, in fact it's rather peculiar German, but we're leaving it.' Actually, I believe that all the existing translations are better than the German original. Finally my German text was translated into Swedish verse by Meschke for the Stockholm Opera production. I have just read the completed French translation, also in verse, by Michel Vittoz, and I am very satisfied with it.

S. Why did you change the names of the characters?

L. The names chosen by Ghelderode are typically French: Videbolle, Salivaine, Basiliquet, etc, but they don't represent anything in another language. I consider that an understanding of the text of *Le Grand Macabre* is essential and that therefore there must be versions in the language of each of the countries where the work is performed, but without changing the names of the characters. I therefore looked for names that could be understood everywhere. Nekrozotar I turned into Nekrotzar, the tsar of the dead: no need to translate, it's clear in every language. Salivaine, the shrewish wife, becomes Mescalina, a combination of the drug Mescalin and Messalina, the virago. The astrologer Videbolle becomes Astradamors, a contraction of Nostradamus together with *mors* and *amor*.

S. Ghelderode's text, like that of the opera, is narrative, but it is a symbolic narration, a fable.

L. Yes, there are several layers to the fable which Ghelderode recounts. The original material derives from an old popular Flemish play, a puppet play, and Ghelderode adapted this material as Goethe did with *Faust*. But he introduced two ideas

116

of his own: on the one hand, although aware of the permanence of death, we cannot prevent ourselves from aspiring to eternal life; on the other hand, Ghelderode shows us, when the end of the world is about to occur, that Nekrotzar, exhausted by pleasure, weakened by over-indulgence in love-making and alcohol, no longer has the strength to accomplish the task of annihilation. Ghelderode's extraordinary idea is the failure of death. I myself have added another idea: if Nekrotzar is really Death, then Death is dead, we have passed into a state of eternal life, we are in Paradise and we have lived through the Last Judgement without realising it. But if Nekrotzar is a charlatan, nothing has changed; he is dead and we have won a reprieve. At the end of the opera, the singers launch into a passacaglia, as in Purcell's *Dido and Aeneas*, and the text of this passacaglia presents the moral of the story: one day we shall die, but we still have a little time at our disposal and we shall take advantage of it to make love, to drink, to take life as it comes. It is an idea that is particularly topical in a civilization where at any moment the whole of humanity may be destroyed. The thought of the threat of collective death is always present but we try to eliminate it from our consciousness and to enjoy to the maximum the days that are left to us.

S.   Can one regard this as a message of hope?

L.   The work is also rather cynical, and I hope human. There's a final element in Ghelderode's play which I haven't used – the local Belgian element. Ghelderode alludes to the rivalry between the Flemings and the Walloons; he himself was Flemish, though he wrote in French, and he hoped for a reconciliation of the two peoples. The reunion of Jusemina and Adrian symbolizes the friendship of the Flemings and the Walloons.

S.   You've said nothing about another dimension which is basic both to Ghelderode and to your opera: the earthiness of the text.

L.   It's a Rabelaisian world, a world full of obscenities, sexual and scatological. People are constantly eating and drinking and leading a very chaotic life. It all happens in a sort of broken-down dictatorship where two opposing parties, both completely corrupt, pursue in reality the same crooked policies. Nothing works but everyone makes the best of things and life is not unpleasant. It's tragic and lighthearted at the same time. For his part, Ghelderode harks back to Brueghel, since the action takes place in Brueghelland, and although he makes no precise reference to them, one is reminded of two Brueghel pictures. In the first, the wine flows like water, grilled ducks fly, half-carved pigs frisk about: it's *The Land of Cockaigne*. The second picture is *The Triumph of Death*: Death arrives on horseback at the head of an army of skeletons who slaughter the living. This Brueghelland can also be said to be the country of Hieronymus Bosch, with its demoniacal and comic cruelties.

S.   Does this background justify the excessively coarse if not obscene language of *Le Grand Macabre* that is unusual in operas?

L.   When people talk about opera, they are referring to grand opera, and there they feel that such language is impossible. But the true tradition of *Le Grand Macabre* is that of fairground theatre, puppet theatre – and that is another reason why I called on Michael Meschke, who is a specialist in puppets. And this mediaeval tradition of the dance of death, which is central to Ghelderode's play, is far older than that of classical or romantic theatre. I have also mentioned strip-cartoons; several cultures are mixed together in *Le Grand Macabre*. Take, for instance, Captain Haddock in *Tintin*; he is constantly hurling insults: 'You macrocephalic baboon!', 'Ectoplasm!', 'Phylloxera!' etc. Captain Haddock is a very proud and very sardonic character, who manipulates the art of insult with great skill. Now in Ghelderode's play the two ministers also insult one another, but I have magnified the insults, turning them into extravagant, Haddock-like insults, incidentally arranged in alphabetical order from A to Z. In the Italian version of *Le Grand Macabre* they used Neapolitan insults which I don't understand very well; they are extraordinarily powerful and more obscene than in the other versions.

S.   Is the obscenity a deliberate provocation?

L.   No, it's not my intention to be provocative, though naturally I enjoy shocking people a bit. But it's a living piece of theatre, and life also means obscenity, excrement, love-making in unorthodox positions. In Stockholm, people thought it was a pornographic piece, but this is untrue.

S.   Do you favour a realistic type of production?

L.   Surrealistic. A semi-realistic, semi-fantastical production. The world of Topor is exactly what I want.

S.   And what role do you assign to the music?

L.   What I'm about to say may seem very arrogant, but I wanted to write a piece in which the characters and situations are really created by the music – as with my ideal trio Monteverdi–Mozart–Verdi. Such a remark is very ambitious and I cannot say whether

118

I have succeeded. Some people have said: 'It isn't Ligeti', but anyone who really knows my work will see that I have remained faithful to my own musical language. In addition, I have introduced stylistic allusions and fragments of pastiche analogous to the *objets trouvés* of pop art, in this case *objets trouvés* in the history of music.

S. Can you give some examples?

L. You take a piece of *foie gras*, you drop it on the carpet and you trample it in until it disappears – that is how I utilize the history of music and especially the history of opera. There are a number of quotations from Schubert and Rameau among others, but they are not detectable.

S. Is this to amuse yourself?

L. Perhaps, but I may add that my aim is a certain degree of anarchic confusion. Incidentally, there are some pseudo-quotations; when I was a student I had to write in different styles – minuets in the style of Haydn or Mozart, rondos in the style of Couperin – and I have gone back to some of these youthful pieces here. You think it's Haydn, but it's Ligeti. They are fake quotations, synthetic quotations. For instance, when the astrologer and his wife Mescalina dance the cancan, there's an allusion to Offenbach's cancan. It's as though you took a steel rod and twisted it. Simultaneously there's Schumann's *Merry peasant* and a pseudo-quotation from Liszt's *Galop chromatique*: one destroys the other. I begin with Offenbach and I end up '*à la Hongroise*'. There's a lot of synthetic folklore.

S. Is it what Bartók calls imaginary folklore?

L. No, because Bartók's imaginary folklore is completely Hungarian, Romanian or Arab, always within the spirit of an existing folklore. In my case, it's a humorous interpolation. My folklore ingredients are impossible, imaginary, unrelated to any specific nation; on the other hand they serve to characterize certain dramatis personae. For instance, for the Chief of the Secret Police, the Gepopo, I concocted a mixture of Brazilian samba and Andalusian flamenco; accompanying Nekrotzar's entry, there is a procession of skeletons from which four musicians detach themselves, each playing a piece of synthetic folklore: the violinist plays a rag in the style of Scott Joplin, an E-flat clarinet embroiders round a flamenco theme, an oboist performs a pseudo-mediaeval hymn in the style of Pérotin, and a piccolo launches into a Hungarian-Scottish pentatonic march. At the same time, off-stage, a bass trumpet plays a distorted samba.

S. The ear doesn't isolate. Only the global result counts and this is made up of collages.

L. Yes, you could say collages. In fact 'Collage' is the title of the orchestral piece I've just described; it also contains a cha-cha-cha played simultaneously in three different tempi. It's a sort of homage to Charles Ives, but I hope that the music nevertheless remains authentic Ligeti. Among these collages, the ostinato bass subject of the last movement of the *Eroica* Symphony also figures, but completely transformed, twisted. All this produces a surrealistic piece, a great mad extravaganza. But the pseudo-quotations are always intended for the comic moments.

S. Would you say that *Le Grand Macabre* in the last resort is made up of alternating comic and lyrical episodes?

L. The alternation is very rapid.

S. And yet sometimes the lyricism predominates.

L. Yes, as for instance at the end of the first scene when, Nekrotzar having departed, the two lovers are left alone and look for a place where they can make love, but are continually disturbed. Then finally they are alone, shut up in the tomb for the rest of the opera, and are totally unaware of the end of the world. When they finally emerge from the tomb, not knowing what has happened, they sing of love. These two characters are always lyrical.

S. Is this lyricism expressed by a sort of leitmotif?

L. No, there are no leitmotifs in my music, but there are what one might call 'leit-characteristics'. The lovers always sing in the same characteristic lyrical style, a bit baroque, a bit Monteverdian. It isn't a pastiche, it is entirely my own music. They are very beautiful and their lyricism is excessive, somehow overblown; they remind me of the two entwined figures who represent the wind in Botticelli's *Birth of Venus*. They are archetypes of lovers. Their musical style is not simply lyrical, it is pretentious-lyrical, extremely ornamented, extremely eloquent, extremely mannered, after the fashion of the etiquette of the Spanish Court. At the end of the opera, when they emerge from the tomb, where they have never stopped making love, they sing the passacaglia in a much more simple style.

S. And what about the ministers?

L. Theirs are spoken parts. They don't sing, they speak in rhythms. At certain moments they use natural speech but the insults are given a very precise rhythmic framework. Each of the characters has his own style. For instance, Prince Go-Go is the only one who always uses recitative. Nekrotzar, the figure of Death (or the charlatan) is very pretentious. He doesn't address anyone directly and, obsessed by his so-called mission, goes on pouring out the same threats; his musical style is very psalmodic. Piet the drunkard has a very ornamented style: he's a buffo tenor. To some extent he's Sancho Panza to Nekrotzar's Don Quixote.

S. How would you characterize the treatment of the voice? How do you reconcile vocal writing and the need to understand the text?

L. Naturally, in the very vocal parts, those allotted to the lovers, there can be no question of understanding the text and it's essential to read the libretto. In a more general sense, people have often spoken of the problems faced by the singers but I don't think it's excessively difficult. In fact it's fairly simple compared to *Aventures*, and in a few years it will have become completely assimilated.

S. Do you use *Sprechgesang*?

L. No, it's so irremediably associated with Schoenberg. Moreover, it conjures up a sort of melodramatism that I don't want. But there is an alternation of sung passages and spoken dialogue. At the outset, for the first Stockholm version, there were long passages of spoken dialogue as in *The Magic Flute* or *Der Freischütz* but I eliminated them to a large extent. Today, eighty per cent of the opera is genuinely sung. As for the level of the difficulties already mentioned, I might add that the only difficult element is the rhythm. However, there is one character whose part is extraordinarily difficult: the Chief of the Secret Police, a part sung by a coloratura soprano who has three arias to sing, the three most difficult arias in the whole history of music, more difficult than Zerbinetta or the Queen of the Night. I was told it was impossible, but on the first night in Stockholm the soprano brought it off. She was Britt-Marie Aruhn, who will also be singing in the Paris Opéra production.

S. What principles did you adopt in the instrumental writing for *Le Grand Macabre*?

L. I did not want to use a big symphony orchestra, in order to avoid giving *Le Grand Macabre* the character of a nineteenth-century opera. On a more practical level, I also had to restrict myself to a scaled-down orchestra in order to leave enough room for a certain number of special instruments: a concert piano, an electric piano, an electric organ, etc. On principle, I never make musical compromises, but I often make technical compromises.

In this case, I had to forgo a large string formation but I kept triple woodwind and quadruple horns and trumpets. The strings, numbering fifteen, have separate and fairly virtuoso parts, as have also the woodwind. As for the percussion, it is entrusted to only three musicians but it involves an immense lay-out and includes a large number of instruments such as sirens and whistles of various kinds, and even motor-car horns (they had already been used by Antheil), twelve of them – no 'series' intended – but each of the three percussionists has two hands and two feet! On the whole, the instrumentation is very colourful, and very virtuoso, especially for the horns, trombones and trumpets.

S. So it's a particularly difficult score presenting all kinds of technical hazards.

L. It's difficult but not impossible. I know very precisely what is possible. In fact at Saarbrücken, in that tiny German theatre, they achieved a remarkably satisfying performance. So it isn't only feasible in the big international theatres. The important thing is goodwill.

S. Have you always met with goodwill?

L. No, not always. But I must say that, up to now, with different conductors, soloists and orchestras, *Le Grand Macabre* has always had good productions. To revert to the orchestral musicians, I may point out that the strings, because of the solo parts allotted to them, become more aware of their responsibilities.

S. What do you remember about the first night of *Le Grand Macabre*?

L. The first performance took place on 12 April 1978, and although it may not be very modest of me to say so, I think it was a great success. There was not the slightest hint of scandal. There were seven performances which were completely sold out and the theatre wanted to put on a second series but it was impossible to organize it. Since then *Le Grand Macabre* has been put on in Hamburg, Saarbrücken, Bologna and Nuremberg. Paris will be the sixth production and London, with the English National Opera, the seventh.

S. What have you learned from these successive productions?

L. Obviously it's always the same music. Here there may be a better singer for a certain role, there for another; but one thing I have learned is that with a mediocre singer the dramatic effect vanishes. The singers are really very important. As for the productions, they have all been different. The Bologna production was the closest to the spirit of the work, the Stockholm one was also remarkable. This is not a criticism of the other productions. At Nuremberg, it was an entirely pop art version with a Marilyn Monroe Venus. Even at Saarbrücken, with fewer technical resources, they achieved a very good result.

S.   Are you sensitive to audience reaction and to bad reviews?

L.   Of course I don't like bad reviews and like everyone else I'm pleased if my work is accepted, but when I'm working I don't think about it, I only think about the music I am writing.

S.   In any case, as far as *Le Grand Macabre* is concerned, the verdict has already been pronounced. Does it make you want to carry on?

L.   Yes. I have already made plans for a new opera in response to a commission from the English National Opera.

S.   I can now imagine your optimistic conclusion. After having succeeded with *Le Grand Macabre* and having seen it through its first productions, I assume that you are less sceptical about contemporary opera?

L.   Perhaps, but I should like to issue one final reservation. I am a composer of today, but *Le Grand Macabre* is linked more closely to tradition than any of my other works. I am aware of the danger of tradition and it's no doubt for this reason that I've never written a symphony. During the past ten years a retro-grade, neo-Romantic, neo-traditionalist movement has de-veloped in Europe and in the United States and I must say quite frankly that I don't like it. Are people now going to say: 'Ligeti is also being *"rétro"* in his opera?' For me, it's just as much a question of production. If *Le Grand Macabre* is staged in the spirit of traditional opera, it becomes conventional. And clearly I don't want that. My strong inclination is towards the fantastical, the exorbitant.

S.   Is the real danger for a composer the temptation to look back or obsession with the avant-garde?

L.   I reject them both. The avant-garde, to which I am said to belong, has become academic. As for looking back, there's no point in chewing over an outmoded style. I prefer to follow a third way: being myself, without paying heed either to categoriza-tions or to fashionable gadgetry.

(1981)   *Translation from French by Terence Kilmartin*

4

Question: In the work of composition what role is played by speculative elements on the one hand and emotional factors on the other?

Answer: Structural features, or speculative patterns, are certainly discernable in my compositions. These are the result of musical deliberations at the time of working the composition out.

However, the initial impulses that set the act of composition going tend to be naïve in character. I imagine the music in the form in which it will later be heard, and hear the piece from beginning to end in my inner ear. To a certain extent what I hear in this way corresponds with what will be heard in performance after the completion of the score – but only to a certain extent. Before this stage is reached, various details will have been modified and refined by structural considerations. These considerations are not an end in themselves. The naïve initial musical idea can be described as music in the raw state. It would be quite possible for the music to be heard in this state – indeed, it is thus heard when I am improvising on the piano – but the sound, measured against the standards I regard as adequate for the structure and form of the piece, is far too primitive.

Structural features, worked out during the process of composition, transform the music from its raw state into a musically consistent and linked network. Composition consists principally of injecting a system of links into naïve musical ideas.

Q. Does this mean that a system, or structural order, is deliberately superimposed on a primitive idea?

A. Not at all. The two categories – musical raw material and structural order – cannot be regarded as distinct and separate areas: it is much truer to say that the linked network, or structural order, corresponds to tendencies already detectable within the raw material itself. The structural potentialities are already contained in the primitive idea, and the act of composition

124

consists mainly of developing these latent potentialities. The difference between a composition in its raw and in its completed state is that, whereas in its raw state the music is not yet fully consistent, the final composition possesses the cohesive qualities of a crystal.

However, the *naïveté* of the raw state is itself not untarnished. It is already interlaced with a series of preferences, and within its amorphousness lie traces of the as yet undiscovered crystal. Music one thinks to be naïve is in fact infected with preconceived likes and dislikes: whatever we do, questions of taste are bound to influence the initial idea. I can without difficulty think up something like a cantilena in 3/4 time, as in *La Traviata*, complete with pizzicato accompaniment, but I consider it neither desirable nor worthwhile to turn such an idea into a composition, since a structure of this type, divorced from its century-old musical context and placed down in a present-day context, would not be consistent.

This example can also be used to make the point that musical consistency is not a matter confined solely to the piece that is actually being composed: there is a historical aspect as well. The structure of a piece of music is relevant only when it is consistent, not merely within the piece itself, but also within the overall historical context of musical construction. I am not suggesting that all that is necessary is to conform: on the contrary, it is only when the individual work brings about some modification of the musical situation as a whole that it justifies its adherence to existing structures.

Q. Are there examples in your own work of this kind of modification?

A. When I was composing *Apparitions* in the latter half of the 1950s, the ideas underlying the music represented a reaction against the musical situation as it was at that time: harmony was in dire danger of toppling over into intervallically neutral and a-harmonic sound structures; rhythmic articulation was in the no less dire danger of toppling over into undifferentiated continuous progressions.

Influenced as I was by revulsion against outworn intervallic and rhythmic patterns and by my wish to bring to the forefront hitherto unexploited musical formulations, such as timbre in its own right, I conjured up in my mind that intricate labyrinth of sound which eventually turned into the orchestral piece mentioned above. In just the same way, revulsion against my own use of neutral harmony and rhythm, on which (as a consequence of *Apparitions*) I built my pieces from *Atmosphères* up to the first two movements of the Requiem, led around 1964 to the abandonment of harmonic neutrality and to the construction of intervallic seed crystals – for example, in the final movement of the Requiem and later, more clearly, in *Lux aeterna* and *Lontano*. It led also, after 1968, to the abandonment of rhythmic neutrality, most consistently in the Second String Quartet.

Q. So it was a case of a double modification, the modification of a modification. On the analogy of minus times minus resulting in plus, could this not be seen as a return to previously abandoned positions? To put it more plainly, was not the abandonment of the abandonment of harmony equivalent to the restitution of harmony?

A. It is of course true that the abolition of non-harmony leads back to harmony. But this newly evolved harmony is not the same as the former harmony – the historical process is irreversible, recurring aspects notwithstanding. The manner in which I use intervals in *Lux aeterna* and *Lontano* reflects my experiences of timbre construction within a harmonically neutral context. That is to say, I treat intervals just as I previously treated timbre complexes. In *Lontano* intervallic structures are subjected to a continual transformation, similar to the transformation of tone colours in *Atmosphères*. The intervals as such are the same as in earlier music, but they are handled in a fundamentally different way: with the sounds of a dead language a new language is being evolved.

For reasons such as these I find myself in a territory in which primary musical ideas and the working out of the composition can no longer be sharply distinguished from one another. The compositional process has been absorbed into the music as conceived directly through the senses, and the raw state already contains traces of the working method. The raw state of which I spoke previously was also not completely raw, since it included a historical pre-shaping. When a composer himself modifies the musical context of a whole era, the work in which this modification occurred exerts an influence over his later ideas, however naïve they may at first appear to be. The primary conception of new pieces contains the imprint of the working processes used in the development of previous pieces. The consequence of this is a feedback effect: the raw state is pre-shaped by experiences gained during composition, and is thus no longer quite 'raw'. The borderline between raw state and finished article becomes fluid, the naïve idea already contains distinct structural features.

Q. So the concept of naïve idea on the one hand and structure on the other is basically false?

A. Despite the fluid borderline there is still a difference. The compositional process can be clearly divided into initial inspiration (i.e., the raw state) and subsequent working out. And, in addition, there is frequently a gap between conception and working out, due to the time lapse – perhaps of several years – that may occur between them.

The feedback relationship has more to do with the fact that during the working out process new musical ideas arise: structural deliberations and naïve idea mutually affect each other. And the working method is itself not just a matter of cold calculation: there are intuitive features in the construction just as there are speculative features in the initial idea. The distinction can be better explained in terms of dosage: the primary musical idea is predominantly intuitive, the working out predominantly speculative. And, just as the musical idea conceived by the senses is pre-shaped by historical associations, so too structural processes and working methods are subject to similar pre-shapings: individual reactions to the working methods of other composers, as well as to one's own working methods in relation to earlier works, lead to a constant modification of constructive principles.

In this connection I might once again cite *Apparitions*. My first version of the music that later became the first movement of this work was sketched in 1956 in Budapest, at which time I knew nothing about serial practices, by then fully developed in Western Europe. When at the beginning of 1957 I went to Cologne and soon got to know the music of Webern as well as that of the post-war generation, I came to realise that the technical and structural standards of my Budapest version were unsatisfactory, measured by Cologne standards. Leaving the initial inspiration untouched, I composed in 1957 a second version, in the working out of which my experiences with serial music were absorbed – I emphasize, my experiences with, not the serial technique itself: I reacted to serial music just as I reacted to my own earlier compositional methods, rejecting it and at the same time building on it, modifying it. Equally dissatisfied with this 1957 version, I composed in 1958 a third version of the movement, this time the definitive one. It was only then that I achieved inner consistency and a sufficiently tight network of structural links. My knowledge of serial music put at my disposal a whole new compositional apparatus, but I was content to regard that just as a *possibility* and made no actual use of it. What I owe to serial music is to a much greater extent an insight into structural relationships and refinements of thought in regard to the subtlest of musical ramifications. A fruitful exchange of ideas with Stockhausen and Koenig proved a decisive factor in my development as a composer, together with a study and analysis of several works by Boulez. It was clear to me from the start that my development would not be along the path of serialism: I was already steeped in compositional assumptions and previous experiences of a totally different kind. The modifications to which my own music was subjected after contact with serialism then exerted their influence, feedback fashion, on serial music itself, producing yet further modifications in its ideas and techniques.

Q. Can you explain, with reference to *Apparitions*, in what way the principles of serialism have been modified?

A. At that time, around 1957, there were two aspects of serial composition that struck me as problematical.

Firstly, the equal status accorded to all musical areas such as pitch, duration, timbre, degree of intensity. The erosion of intervallic relationships, that is to say, of harmony of any kind, and the consequent reduction of intervallic distinctions, persuaded me initially to dispense with intervals as structural components. I composed sound webs of such density that the individual intervals within them lost their identity and functioned simply as collective interval groups, no longer as separate intervals. However, this meant that the pitch function had also been eliminated: series based on pitch had become meaningless, and their place in the structural pattern was taken by internal relationships of motion and an intricate network of parts. Pitches and intervals now had a purely global function as aspects of compass and note density. There is no serial organization of pitches in *Apparitions*. And by such means the entire basis of serial music – that is to say, the equal status of all musical elements – has been nullified.

The other aspect of serial composition I found problematical was the organization of all the musical elements within a unified plan. In serial music it was axiomatic that a single basic order should be manifest throughout the various areas. There was also a recognizable tendency to regard a pitch series as the starting point, and to arrange the other elements in accordance with that, even to the extent that the notes as arranged in a series would initially be given numbers. These numbers would then be detached from the pitch series and applied to the areas of duration, timbre, intensity, and later even to wider determining factors such as density, compass, proportions of structural detail, etc. One could also work the other way round: a series of numbers or of numerical relationships – ratios for instance – would be laid down and then applied to the various musical areas. Uniformity of organization was the fundamental tenet of serial music: a quantifiable basic order, a modulus, had to be laid down, and every single part of the composition had to be derivable from the chosen modulus.

I did not see any necessity for this kind of unified treatment of all the elements. Indeed, I detected in it a discrepancy: quantification applied equally within the various areas produced, from the point of view of our perception and understanding of musical processes, radically different effects, so that there was no guarantee that a single basic order would produce analogous structures on the various levels of perception and understanding. On the contrary, adherence to a single basic order led to structures that seemed incompatible. Unity remained fixed at the level of commentary, a verbal description of the composition: it was clapped on the musical events from the outside, and had no direct impact on our minds.

In his essay 'Wie die Zeit vergeht' (*Die Reihe* 3) Stockhausen had pointed out, in connection with Boulez's *Structures I*, the arbitrary co-ordination of an additively constructed duration series (derived from the multiplication of a fundamental duration value) with a pitch series that had not come about by additive means, but was rather akin to a logarithmic progression. Unlike Stockhausen, however, I felt that, even when pitches on the one hand and duration values on the other were governed by the same quantitative regulation – a logarithmic progression, say – the analogy between the two series existed only on the level of verbal description. There was no musically effective analogy, since our nervous system reacts to pitch relationships and duration relationships in fundamentally different ways, and the two areas, though sharing a common context physically, are separated from one another by our diverging ways of responding to them. From a study of physics I *know* that fifth and fundamental tone stand in a frequency ratio of 3:2. I also *know* that frequency is the equivalent of speed, that is to say, it represents the number of vibrations within a chosen period of time. This knowledge has been acquired through experiments in physics, with the help of a measuring apparatus. When I hear a fifth, however, I *feel* a certain acoustical quality, my sensory perceptions convey no impression of speed, and the ratio of 3:2 (the physical definition of a fifth) plays no part in my understanding. Meanwhile I am accepting without question simple duration relationships as recognizable quantitative elements within a speed range accessible to my perceptions. A simultaneous combination of triplet and duplet, for example, appears directly to my understanding as a time factor of 3:2, without the help of a measuring apparatus. By contrast, it is hardly necessary to point out that those physical speeds which are perceived by my ears in the form of pitches lie (as far as my nervous system is concerned) not in the physical realm of speed, but in an area of the mind in which perceptions are qualitative, not quantitative. For this reason a basic order that postulates a ratio of $a:b$ as a regulating factor common to both pitch and duration (or speeds) is irrelevant, indeed meaningless in relation to a musical structure, which in structural terms reflects mental rather than physical processes. The $a:b$ ratio in the realm of pitch is only *physically*, not *mentally*, analogous to the $a:b$ ratio in the realm of duration or speed.

The discrepancy in the serial outlook lies above all in the unmotivated equation of the physical and mental levels of approach.

I can perhaps make this clearer through a comparison with painting. The colours used in a picture play a significant part in producing an effect on our minds. In physical terms, however, the effect of each colour is the result of the chemical combination of certain dyes. As far as the picture itself is concerned, the chemical composition of the dye is of no immediate relevance, for the colour structure of the picture and the chemical structure of the dye exist on two different planes. The second plane may of course be dependent on the first, but the nature of each is different. I paint with white, the effect 'white' is produced by a certain arrangement of lead and oxygen atoms or of zinc and oxygen atoms, but in regard to the picture it is only the effect 'white' that is significant, not the question whether the dye contains atoms of zinc or lead. In place of zinc and lead atoms one could speak of crystal lattices, electron orbits, light absorption, and so on – each plane has another plane beneath it – but I am painting *directly* with white and only indirectly with crystal lattices.

To return to music: in working out a notional compositional structure the decisive factor is the extent to which it can make its effect directly on the sensory level of musical perception.

Q. Have these considerations led you to a complete rejection of serial principles?

A. I have been talking about modifications, not total abandonment. Apart from these problems of equal status, analogical form and unification, there are aspects of serial thinking that I have felt to be promising for the development of my own working methods, above all, the principle of selection and systemization of elements and procedures, as well as the principle of consistency: postulates, once decided on, should be carried through logically, but only in those areas in which they are musically relevant. Arising from this, I did find it feasible – while rejecting a uniform treatment of *all* postulates – to build a compositional structure consisting of a heterogeneous repertory of elements. The timbre structure, for instance, could be made to conform to regulations quite different from those governing the rhythmic structure. All that was necessary was to ensure that elements and procedures, once tested and fixed, would then be applied completely and consistently in the area in which their viability had been proved. In this way my compositional working method could be regarded in a very general sense as serial, though not a single series had been employed.

Q. Serial music without a series: a contradiction in terms?

A. The remark is simply an attempt to find a dividing line capable of definition. My compositional approach might no longer be recognizable as genuine 'serial music', but within it thought processes and methods of working whose roots lay in serial music were preserved.

As an example let me describe some technical aspects of the first movement of *Apparitions*. There are no true series in this, but there are predetermined formulae in the areas of rhythm, dynamics, timbre, pitch, compass, note density, character of motion, formal articulation. There is no single order governing all these areas together: the rhythmic relationships, for instance, are different from the dynamic relationships, and so on. But a relative unity is achieved through the manner in which the various areas are linked together, similar to a machine, which contains various components such as wheels, cogs, axles, belts, etc, the very diversity of which enables the whole apparatus to function as a unit. In the area of rhythm, for example, there is a quasi-serial repertory of duration elements: a shortest element and a longest, and between these two extremes a stipulated number of duration elements of varying length. (Since I am dealing here simply with matters of principle, I shall not go into detail concerning the ratio of these durations to one another, the number of elements involved, etc.) These duration elements of varying length are not arranged in a series, nor is there any parity in regard to the frequency of their occurrence. Thus one of the main postulates of serial thinking – that all elements, no matter how selected, must occur with equal frequency – has been disregarded. There are more of the shorter duration elements than of the longer ones, and the longest of all is used only once. There is, however, a system of apportionment of duration elements: the length of the shortest element, multiplied by the number of times it appears in the piece, matches the total length of the longest element. A similar process is followed with the other elements: the shorter an element, the more frequently it occurs, and vice versa. The duration multiplied by frequency of occurrence produces a constant.

Q. What is the purpose of this apportionment of duration elements? What are its advantages as compared with a duration series? To what extent is this apportionment musically relevant?

A. If one constructs a piece on the basis of a duration series in which every element of the series should appear with equal frequency, the longest duration element must of necessity occur as often within the complete composition as the shortest duration element. This results in an over-emphasis on the longer duration elements, establishing a hierarchy that is contrary to the a-hierarchical principle of serial music. A pitch series, a twelve-note series, for example, is structured a-hierarchically, for no note carries greater weight than another; a duration series, on the other hand, is of its very nature hierarchical, for, given an equal number of shorter and longer duration elements, the longer values predominate in terms of time.

The discrepancy between duration and pitch series rests on the basic difference of our perceptions in regard to duration and pitch: the former we interpret in the main quantitatively, the latter qualitatively. Recognizing to what extent the longer values predominated, Boulez split up the duration elements in his *Structure Ib*, combining the series arrangement with a second articulation based on Messiaen's technique of rhythmic cells. This was a useful procedure, since it reduced the over-emphasis of the long values.

All the same, I asked myself why there should be a duration series at all, when its elements are in any case split up to such an extent that the serial arrangement is no longer discernible in the structure of the piece. Could one not start out with a structural basis of a different type – one that allowed the rhythmic structure to emerge directly from the basic order without the complication of a *second* order cancelling out the first? That brought me to the idea of setting up a *repertory* of duration elements in place of a fixed duration series.

The prototype for a repertory of this sort might be the letter-case used by printers when setting by hand. One compartment of this case contains a certain number of the letter 'a', the second the letter 'b', and so on. Each letter of the alphabet is represented, but not in equal numbers; there are more examples of 'a' and 'e' than there are of 'k' and 'm', for instance, and again more of these than of 'x' and 'z'. That is to say, the letters that occur most frequently in the written language are more fully represented in their compartments than those occurring less frequently. In the first movement of *Apparitions* the repertory of duration elements is laid out in a manner similar to a letter-case: the 'compartment' of the shortest duration values contains the largest number of 'letters'; in the final 'compartment', containing the longest value, there is only a single 'letter'. The rhythmic language of this music consequently makes more frequent use of the short values than of the long ones: in my conception of the overall form I had the idea of a static and rhythmically balanced shape, balance in this case meaning that neither long nor short elements should predominate.

Of course, the apportionment of duration elements according to a frequency constant is valid only for this one piece. For other pieces with different rhythmic characteristics it would have been possible to plan completely different methods of apportionment. (I did in fact make use of this repertory principle in the electronic piece *Artikulation*, but in that piece the product of duration value and frequency was not a constant.)

The letter-case system fulfilled yet another purpose. In it were contained the elements, their numbers and their apportionment, but what was not predetermined was the method of linking these elements together. Thus I was free to make use of a syntactic system independent of the repertory. The drawback of a series is that it determines in advance both the elements and the means of linking them together, whereas the repertory principle allows for a division into two separate working phases: selection of elements *and* setting up of a syntax.

It would go too far to maintain that this is always an advantage: for instance, the repertory system would be inadequate for musical patterns that are a-syntactic. Rather one might say that the repertory system and the musical syntax it enabled me to employ were, as far as my compositional intentions were concerned, more fruitful than an adherence to strict serial thinking would have been – at least, during one particular working period in the latter part of the 1950s. In later pieces, from about 1960 onwards, I made further modifications in the method described here, working less and less with a predetermined repertory of elements, but rather with predetermined syntactic systems or with linked networks (particularly in and following my orchestral piece *Atmosphères*). Because of this, the first working phase (the selection of elements) has become of decreasing relevance, while what was originally the second phase, the setting up of a musical syntax, has taken over the main role.

Q. In connection with the first movement of *Apparitions* you spoke of balance. Is this an ideal to be pursued in relation to form?

A. Not at all. Balanced, or static forms are only *one* among many other forms in which I have composed. To the static type belong the orchestral pieces *Atmosphères* and *Lontano*, to mention only the most characteristic examples. Equilibrium, the apparent suspension of the formal process, 'extended time' – these qualities are applied in a more consequent manner in these pieces than in *Apparitions* (although I regard the first movement of *Apparitions* as the key piece, since this movement marked my change of style).

But I have also worked with dynamic, restless, fragmented forms, as for example in *Aventures*, *Nouvelles Aventures* and in the third movement of the Requiem. If the form of *Atmosphères* can be said to be characterized by musical *states* (in contrast to my earlier music, which consisted mainly of *occurrences*), in works such as *Aventures* a number of contrasted musical states are superimposed on or interlocked with each other. The music is not 'occurrent' in these pieces either, but its static nature is cancelled out by the method of interlocking its various states. The changes of state occur as a rule abruptly: one of the commonest expression marks in these particular scores is 'stop suddenly, as if broken off'.

Q. Are the two categories of form – static (situational) and split (interlocked) – to be seen as extremes, or can there be a synthesis between them?

A. The two categories are indeed mutually exclusive, but not in all respects. The fact that compositions such as *Aventures* are based on 'states', though these are of short duration and are continually giving way to other 'states', establishes a certain relationship between the two types. Thus the question of synthesis does not arise, for the static form is already contained within the split (or interlocked) one.

However, I have worked with yet further types of form. For example, the type labelled 'like a precision mechanism' is characterized by a specific rhythmical configuration: a state is represented in terms, not of a 'smooth', but of a 'fine-ground' continuity, so that the music is seen as if through a number of superimposed lattices. Compositions of this type include the piece for harpsichord *Continuum*, the third movement of the Second String Quartet and the third movement of the Chamber Concerto. The earliest example of this 'lattice' music is my *Poème symphonique* for 100 metronomes (1962).

In addition to these, there is the 'kaleidoscopic' type. In compositions in this category the elements are separate and contrasted musical shapes, which together make up a kind of repertory, on lines similar to the 'letter-case' principle. Here, however, the 'elements' are not pure ones, since they have already been moulded into shapes. In the composition they are combined each time in different ways, exactly like the particles of a kaleidoscope, that always retain their own identity, but, when shuffled, produce different patterns. My *Ten Pieces for Wind Quintet* are based entirely on this kaleidoscopic principle, and I have used it too in the Second String Quartet and in the Chamber Concerto though in these pieces it is obscured by other types, such as the static and interlocked forms.

Q. Is a variety of different methods being employed in the compositional technique as well as in the course of working out the composition as a whole?

A. The methods vary from piece to piece, as I have already indicated, and also by degrees: experiences with one piece lead to modifications in technique in the next, and each new piece raises further questions of a technical nature that are dealt with in ensuing pieces, these leading in turn to further questions.

I spoke, in connection with the first movement of *Apparitions*, about the repertory principle and the linking technique, both of which are extensions of the serial idea. In the second movement of this same work, however, I made no further use of a repertory of duration values, nor indeed did I use a repertory of elements of any kind. All the same, the repertory principle was just as valid for the second movement as for the first, with the difference that this time it was not the elements themselves, but the deployment of these elements that was organized according to a repertory or 'letter-case' system. In place of letters, the case contained schemata for links and types of motion.

To put it more clearly: the 'letters' used in the construction of the first movement were contained within the compartments of the letter-case, but the rules for linking them together lay outside it. In the construction of the second movement, the rules for linking were themselves inside the letter-case, while outside was a syntactic system of a higher order, determining in which way the links would be deployed. The principle of *linking links together* made possible the evolvement of that closely woven musical network which is characteristic of the second movement of *Apparitions*. For translation into perceptible music this imaginary and abstract constructional network called for a web of actual instrumental sounds, and so it was necessary to divide up the score into a large number of individual parts, though, as far as hearing them was concerned, these individual parts were completely submerged in the overall texture.

Such was the origin of 'inaudible' polyphony, or *micro-polyphony*, in which each single part, though imperceptible by itself, contributes to the character of the polyphonic network as a whole. In other words, the individual parts and the musical configurations arising from these parts remain subliminal, but each part and each configuration is, in relation to the overall structure, transparent in the sense that all changes in detail lead to changes, however slight, in the total effect.

In the next piece I composed, *Atmosphères*, I made further extensions of micro-polyphony: the network became even more refined, the remnants of independent rhythmic shapes were eliminated, and micro-polyphony was used to bring about gradual transformations of timbre and texture. It is true that in subsequent pieces composed during the '60s I made modifications in my method of working with micro-polyphony, but on the whole I stayed loyal to the conception. In my works from about 1966 onwards I began to thin out the dense polyphonic network: for example, in the second movement of the Cello Concerto, and even more radically in the works after 1968. The individual parts were still more or less subliminal, but now and again there emerged musical shapes at a level of the individually perceptible. Typical of this thinned-out micro-polyphony – now resembling the transparency of a drawing rather than the opaqueness of a painting – are the Second String Quartet (composed 1968) and the Chamber Concerto for thirteen players (composed 1969–70). One might say that the micro-polyphony of these pieces has become less 'micro', the musical texture being balanced on the threshold between imperceptible musical factors and others which are perceptible as shapes.

I had the feeling that I was remaining true to micro-polyphony, however much I had been modifying it. But with the mounting number of modifications there did come a point at which these modifications began to assume more weight than the original condition itself.

In my orchestral piece of Summer 1971, *Melodien*, the polyphony is no longer 'micro', yet the texture of this piece does not suggest a reversion to earlier techniques. It can rather be seen as the logical outcome of micro-polyphony, though containing no micro-polyphonic movement in the literal sense of the word. The situation is similar to that which prevailed after the abandonment of serial music. Series no longer existed, yet nonetheless post-serial music bore within itself traces of experiences gained in working with serial techniques. It was not a retreat to a previous phase, but an advance towards a new style and a new structural concept. My musical position following the abandonment of micro-polyphony is similar: there pass through my mind inter-linked parts of a melodic character, a polyphonic network in which not all the individual parts are submerged. On the contrary, the melodically shaped parts retain their individuality, they move simultaneously at varying speeds and possess a melodic and rhythmic line of their own, varying from and independent of the other parts. In this way melodic shape, that forbidden fruit of modern music, can to some extent be restored.

(1971)   *Translation from German by Geoffrey Skelton*

LIST OF COMPOSITIONS

(Incomplete for the period 1941 to 1956)

1941	*Kineret* for mezzosoprano and piano
1940–50	*Ballade und Tanz* for school orchestra
1951–53	*Musica Ricercata*, 11 pieces for piano
1953	Six Bagatelles for Wind Quintet
1953–54	String Quartet No.1 *Métamorphoses nocturnes*
1955	*Night* and *Morning* for unaccompanied choir
1956	*Víziók* for orchestra
1957	*Glissandi*, electronic composition
	Apparitions, version for string orchestra with harp, piano, harpsichord and percussion
1958	*Artikulation*, electronic composition
1958–59	*Apparitions* for orchestra (final version)
1961	*Atmosphères* for orchestra
	Trois Bagatelles for piano
	Fragment for chamber orchestra
	Die Zukunft der Musik (a happening)
1961–62	*Volumina* for organ
1962	*Poème symphonique* for 100 metronomes
	Aventures for 3 singers and 7 instrumentalists
1962–65	*Nouvelles Aventures* for 3 singers and 7 instrumentalists
1963–65	Requiem for soprano and mezzosoprano solo, two choirs and orchestra
1966	*Lux aeterna* for 16-part unaccompanied chorus
	Cello Concerto
	Aventures & Nouvelles Aventures: stage version
1967	*Lontano* for orchestra
	Etude No.1 for organ, *Harmonies*
1968	*Continuum* for harpsichord
	String Quartet No.2
	Ten Pieces for Wind Quintet
1968–69	*Ramifications* for string orchestra, or 12 solo strings

1969	Etude No.2 for organ, *Coulée*
1969–70	Chamber Concerto for 13 instrumentalists
1971	*Melodien* for orchestra
1972	Double Concerto for flute, oboe and orchestra
1972–73	*Clocks and Clouds* for 12-part women's chorus and orchestra
1973–74	*San Francisco Polyphony* for orchestra
1974–77	*Le Grand Macabre*, opera in 2 acts
1976	*Monument, Selbstportrait, Bewegung*, 3 pieces for 2 pianos
1978	Scenes and Interludes from *Le Grand Macabre* for soprano, mezzosoprano, tenor and baritone solo, chorus (ad lib) and orchestra
	Hungarian Rock for harpsichord
	Passacaglia ungherese for harpsichord
1982	Trio for violin, horn and piano
1982	*Drei Phantasien* for 16-part unaccompanied chorus, after poems of Friedrich Hölderlin
1983	*Magyar Etüdök* (Hungarian Studies) for unaccompanied chorus after poems of Sándor Weöres
	Piano Concerto